HOW TO HAVE
MAGNIFICENT
SEX

THE 7 DIMENSIONS OF A VITAL SEXUAL CONNECTION

LANA L. HOLSTEIN, M.D.

D1507176

THREE RIVERS PRESS
NEW YORK

Published by Three Rivers Press, New York, New York.
Member of the Crown Publishing Group, a division of Random House, Inc.
www.randomhouse.com

THREE RIVERS PRESS and the tugboat design are registered trademarks of
Random House, Inc.

Originally published in hardcover by Harmony Books, a division of Random
House, Inc., New York, in 2001.

Printed in the United States of America

Design by Barbara Balch

Library of Congress Cataloging-in-Publication Data
Holstein, Lana.
    How to have magnificent sex : the 7 dimensions of a vital
sexual connection / Lana Holstein.
        1. Sex instruction.   2. Sex instruction for women.
    3. Man-woman relationships.   4. Intimacy (Psychology).
    5. Sex—Handbooks, manuals, etc.   I. Title.
    HQ56 .H65   2001
    613.9'6—dc21

                                                    00-058160

ISBN 1-4000-4981-4

10 9 8 7 6 5 4 3 2

First Paperback Edition

TO DAVID:

My Mate, my Sensual Explorer,
my Man, my "Corazon," my Confidant,
my Soul Mate, my Beloved,
MAY OUR ELECTRIC CONNECTION NEVER CEASE.

Contents

Testimonials

Testimonials of what men and women workshop attendees have said was most important about Dr. Holstein's workshop:

"Learning that sex gives me energy is incredible—I'll never be too tired again!"

"My excellent and wonderful thirty-year marriage has received a sexual awakening. A great marriage is going to become even greater."

"I tapped into a spiritual and physical energy I didn't know existed. My discomfort with the dispassion of sexual pleasure has been replaced with a language that is open, honest, and loving."

"Mark and I would like to thank you and David for showing us the path to deeper intimacy. We found all aspects of your program to be excellent. You and David have a unique ability to present delicate matters in a totally comfortable, open format. Your seminar has taken Mark and me to a new level of connectedness, and we will always be grateful to you for this."

"Learning to interact on a more nonverbal basis was very important, as well as learning how to use energy and meditation techniques to personally release old habits."

"Reconnecting intimacy with my husband, seeing him as I did twenty years ago. And feeling a sense of loving and being loved on a very deep level."

"The workshop changed the way we look at each other and our relationship. Its emphasis on the person and the connection—not the sex as a goal. Technique becomes incidental and outcome unimportant. Lovemaking reached a whole different dimension and frees up the relationship so each partner can just 'be.'"

"Your workshop very likely turned our relationship around."

Acknowledgments

As a virgin in the book-writing experience I have had gentle guidance in the process of transferring my discoveries about the sexual connection onto the printed page. Billie Fitzpatrick was absolutely essential in the creative process, helping me clarify the dimensions innumerable times so they carried to the reader the same energy I had witnessed in my office. Without her this book would not exist.

Debra Goldstein provided tremendous instruction and support as my agent, teaching the basics in taking a concept from mental construct to print. She has been a wonderful ally from the time she read of the dimensions and said, "Of course!"

Shaye Areheart, my editor at Harmony Books, was always enthusiastic. She understood my ideas and put her wonderful experience and expertise behind them. Many thanks to her, as well as to her assistant, Vivian Fong.

To the patients who have shared their private lives with me—their wounds, dreams, and challenges—I bow in appreciation. Their identities have been completely disguised, but their stories live on in my heart and soul.

Women help women, and friends help friends; I have been blessed with both during this initiation. Since the beginning, Alinda Carole Page has been a steadfast supporter of my belief that sexual fulfillment is a birthright for all of us. She has always understood even when others have not. She has been a colleague, a deep friend, and the sharer of profound experiences.

My thanks also extend to the Tucson girls—Suzanne Kaiser, Kathleen Johnson, and Holly McCarter—for all the wild stories, the laughs, the birthdays, and for being goddesses of "power-lounging." And I appreciate my children, Natalie and Nicholas, for putting up with a mother who writes and lectures about sex.

Enid and Mel Zuckerman, Gary Frost, and Jerry Cohen have provided unwavering support and a gorgeous environment for expanding my work in sexuality at Canyon Ranch. Thank you. I am also thankful for the support of innumerable professionals and friends at the Ranch who have gently teased me for always talking about sex; but most especially I am thankful to Nancy Inskeep, R.N., who handles all with great grace.

Dianne Dunkelman, Kathy De Laura, and all the women at Speaking of Women's Health receive not only my kudos for their wonderful "edutainment" of women but my thanks for their support over and over again.

I am thankful to Jock McKeen and Bennett Wong for stimulating me to think about the dimensions of sexuality even though we did not agree on the existence of spiritual sex. My deep appreciation extends as well to Lorna and Phil Sarrel, Yale Med School professors, who so long ago sparked my commitment to sexuality consultation which is now my greatest passion.

Finally, David Taylor, you are the catalyst to all that I know in my body and soul about sex. Without your insightful mind, your willingness to put our relationship out there, but, most of all, your deep, sustaining love of me in all dimensions, this would be just a bunch of ideas instead of a magnificent reality.

HOW TO HAVE MAGNIFICENT SEX

1

Finding the Magic of a Passionate Connection

THE MAGIC IS MULTIDIMENSIONAL

Think about the last time you made love. Were you making love or having sex? Did your bodies blend into a sweet sensual wholeness suffused with exquisite energy and pleasure? Did you feel the power of your desire for your man or woman merge with the precious connection of your hearts? Did you really let go, sharing the wild ecstasy of the moment without limits?

Or, was your body connected but your mind wandering? Maybe it was reliving unpleasant business dealings, or surveying the to-do list. "Now let's see, I have to go to the cleaners, stop by the store . . ."

So often during lovemaking we are not really there, or our body is there but the rest of us has disengaged. Even if we have overcome the resistance to initiating sex, afterward the effort to have it does not seem worth the lonely, mechanical connection. How often during sex do we close our eyes to the unfocused look of our partner and concentrate on achieving an orgasm, only to feel physically relieved but mentally bored by the encounter? Is this all there is? How did sex become so mechanical, uninteresting, and hollow? How can we revive the spark, access the lust, and unlock our sexual spirit? How can we make sex all that it is meant to be?

In twenty-five years of counseling people on sexuality as part of my medical practice, and most recently in my position as the medical director of women's health at Canyon Ranch Health Resort, I have had the opportunity to speak to thousands of women and men about their sexual dissatisfaction. I have listened to the countless sexual concerns of all types of people—car mechanics, university professors, homemakers, financiers, artists, and builders—and I have heard a resounding cry for some way out of this pall of sexual mediocrity. And the sexual-technique books and the magazine articles do not solve the problems I see. Our heads are given sex tidbits and clever ideas to spice up our intimate lives; however, we know in our bones something is still missing. Sexuality unfortunately is often mediocre in a land of superlatives and boring in the face of our fast-paced, overstimulated lives. In fact, we do not need more data, we need to change our fundamentally flawed view of sexuality.

What is needed is a view of the multidimensional nature of our sexual connection. When couples realize that sex takes place on many levels, when each partner begins to value the other's strengths, and when they both begin to include all the dimensions in their sexual encounters, the tapestry of sex comes alive. I have seen men and women who have sex only on one dimension; perhaps they are lustful, they really know how to "do" each other, but where is the heart, the intimacy, the soul? Or, there are partners who have a deep, abiding love for each other, but no fire, no desire, sparks their connection. Then there are the couples who fight over who is "right" about sex, whose approach to sex is better or more moral, meaningful, or magical. Now sex becomes a game of power, where one person gets his or her way and the other gives in.

None of these connections explores the true depth of sex or its ability to transform our relationships. We are settling, negotiating, compromising, because we have never been presented with the alternative, a sexual connection that is powerful and exquisite, desire-filled and dignified. Cultivating such a multidimensional relationship is not difficult, it is just new. The dimensional perspective puts life into the humdrum of a long marriage and depth into a new connection. It is an approach that applauds change as well as the strengths each man or woman brings to sex, and it finally acknowledges our sexual complexity by considering that we are sexually involved with our lover at seven levels or dimensions. Multidimensional sex is the ultimate aphrodisiac, potent, accessible, ever-changing.

I know that sex can be reenergized: it has happened during the workshops and sessions on sexuality at Canyon Ranch. It has happened in my own wonderful marriage and in many other relationships I have had the privilege to know. It is something that can happen for you as well. Good sex is not just a wish or the "icing on the cake": it is a fundamental pillar in a solid relationship.

If your sexual life is not what you desire, you are not alone. Judging from the latest surveys about sex in America, our most intimate connection has become not only mediocre and unsatisfying, but stultifying and dismal. Thirty-three percent of women said they did not want sex, and just as many men said they had persistent problems climaxing early. Hmmm. Wonder if there could be some connection! Twenty-five percent of women do not have orgasms, and 14 percent of men say they have no interest in sex. Overall, 43 percent of women and 31 percent of men say they have problems with sex.

These statistics have become a hot topic of discussion in recent years because they reveal the truth of what really happens—or more aptly, does not happen—behind bedroom doors. I am not surprised. From my many years as a sexuality counselor I am very aware that many people have stopped looking for the true depth of sex and have abandoned the belief in its ability to transform our relationships.

Couples frequently describe a strange awkwardness that develops around initiating sex. They feel almost shy or hesitant about being erotic with one another. Instead of risking disturbing the calm surface of the relationship by asking for more or for something different sexually, many settle for a polite but increasingly celibate roommate arrangement. Others continue to be sexually active, but the sex remains mechanical and uninteresting. Many women and men don't even know how to bring up the subject of sex, much less how to fix or heal the problem. We have too easily let go of our hope for magical, passionate sex.

Unfortunately, in the typical relationship, this sexual disappointment leads to conflict or to boredom, and of course sexual encounters become less frequent. Close, nurturing sexual connections now become a rare commodity. You know how it is. Life interferes with sexual intimacy. There are highly demanding careers. There are highly demanding children. There are incessant "shoulds" that devour precious pieces of unstructured time, time that might have led to spontaneous, passionate lovemaking. Distance replaces closeness.

So, what do we do when we are stuck sexually? Some people turn to the virtual sex of the Internet; some feed the billion-dollar pornography industry; some just quietly give up, believing that sex was a passing initial phase of their relationship. Sexual alienation and dysfunction are entrenched in our society, causing a vast yearning for creative, powerful sexual connection without any map to the treasure.

Take a look at your own sexual beliefs. No matter what the current state of your sexual life is, do you still believe that ecstatic sex is possible? Or do you get trapped into thinking that it's only for the young, for the first stage of a love relationship? And then sadly believe that when the honeymoon is over, we are destined for a life of mediocre sex, unless perhaps we go outside of the relationship in search of someone new to create the spark?

Determined to come up with a solution for all of these common sexual dilemmas, I have analyzed and deciphered, researched and systematized the accounts of sex as it happens day to day for most of us. And from these both short-term and long-lasting encounters with women and men of varying backgrounds and ages, I have developed a dynamic approach to sexual fulfillment that not only answers the important sexual questions, but also explains sexual reluctance and boredom and gives back the power to have wonderful, passionate, ecstatic sex.

The approach presented in this book gives you the map. Sex is not mysterious; rather, it suffers from having never been approached systematically. If you wanted to play better tennis or golf, you would take lessons, practice, think about your swing, and invest some time and attention on becoming more skillful. Why not look at sexual expertise in the same way? Study your strengths and weaknesses, practice new levels of connecting, learn a system that makes you the best lover that you can be. This approach is not difficult but it does require self-honesty. It is not exclusive to new or long-term relationships, but it does require putting sex out on the table between you and your partner. Finally, women and men who use the seven dimensions will feel a more intense sexual connection with their lover and a renewed belief in the wonderful potential of magnificent sex.

My entire philosophy or approach to sex is rooted in the idea that sex is not just about lust or desire; it's not just about emotional intimacy or love. It's about all these factors and more. Specifically, I have determined that the best sexual relationships contain seven components or dimensions. When all seven dimensions are aligned and energized, the relationship is healthy, fulfilling, and stimulating and possesses the potential to always be fun, passionate, even ecstatic. These seven dimensions create and maintain the dynamic connection between two people. However, when one or more of these dimensions becomes stagnant or loses its energy, the sexual relationship is affected and one or both partners feel dissatisfied.

This book thus proposes a fundamental shift in the way we approach sex. It calls you to explore your sexual strengths and weaknesses so that you can maximize your sexual potential. It provides a systematic approach to your sexual life in order to clarify which dimensions already work for you and your partner and which dimensions need to be developed. It will teach you facts, let you learn by example, and push you to reconsider your sexual "rules." It will ask you to explore your vulnerabilities in order to understand why a particular dimension may be difficult for you. It will help you to acknowledge your partner's strengths as you build a fabulous sex life together. It will guide you to the magic and wonder of discovering the spiritual dimension of sex—the most profound connection that lovers can experience.

Magnificent Sex takes you on a journey of exploration where you are a traveler not a tourist, a participant not an observer. This book provides a clear description of how to have multidimensional sex. It offers profiles of couples using the multidimensional approach, illuminating how women and men gain the insight and learn the tools that lead to magnificent sex. It will give you an understandable path to the mystery of claiming and nurturing exciting and vibrant sex.

In many ways, the seven dimensions of sexual connection will resonate with a deep familiarity. They just make sense. They are a natural and fundamental element to our connection with our partner, and without them, the very fabric of a relationship will weaken or tear. Essentially, the dimensions of sexual connection are based on innate, organic features of our humanity. Here are the seven dimensions and their goals:

▶ The biologic dimension shows you how to make your body function at its sexual peak.

▶ The sensual dimension increases your capacity to feel sexual pleasure.

▶ The desire dimension frees you from inhibitions and refuels your lust for each other.

▶ The heart dimension enriches your love and commitment and strengthens your connection to your partner.

▶ The intimacy dimension builds trust and open communication and infuses your connection with vitality and depth.

▶ The aesthetic dimension uncovers your inner radiance and creates a pathway to your sexual soul.

▶ The transpersonal dimension teaches you how to merge with your partner at the level of the soul and transcend the mundane and become one.

Each of these dimensions has a positive pole, the aspect of the dimension that is energized, powerful, and fulfilling. Each dimension also has a negative, destructive, or uncomfortable pole. Finally, the magnetic charge between these two extremes is often neutralized in the middle, or static, place. Here is where couples often feel stuck in a particular dimension. They feel they have reached a stalemate, an accommodation of each other's approach to sex, rather than any synergy of sexual energy. As you go through the seven dimensions and read the true-life anecdotes, look for your own patterns. For each aspect of the sexual interaction determine your and your partner's position. Are you at the positive end of the scale in the desire dimension, or the negative? Have you become stuck in the middle of the heart dimension where you are mainly showing a "stingy heart" to your lover? Seeing where you are on the spectrum opens the door to change. Then using the tools helps you to shift the beliefs and behaviors that have kept you stuck and your sex life stagnant.

Remember, you want a multidimensional *relationship*. So, do not expect to be perfect in all aspects. It is perfectly normal for one of you to be strong in the intimacy or heart dimensions, for example, while the other has the desire and sensual handled. Or, maybe you will find that you both score high in a particular area and can revel in your sexual expertise. The goal is to have all the dimensions represented in your connection.

Throughout a couple's relationship, the issues they have with the seven dimensions can change; indeed, we are in constant flux—some of us more dramatically than others. When women hit menopause, for instance, they often experience a remarkable shift in their relationship to their own body, as well as in their sexual desire, or libido. This can also be true of men who are aging. So, return to this book as your relationship matures, or as you age or even if you have a new lover, in order to craft the sexual interaction that you desire.

Maybe you will recognize yourself in some of the examples that identify themes I've seen over and over in my practice. Maybe you will determine that your partner is a champ in a particular dimension and you've never realized how little attention you give to this aspect of lovemaking. As you read about the common blocks in each sexual area, you will understand many of the underlying beliefs and experiences that cause problems. If you do not have a partner right now, you can still benefit from looking at all the chapters so that you can begin to create a framework for your next relationship. When we know what we want, we are much more likely to get it!

Use the chapters on each dimension as you wish. If you feel confident about your sexual skills and pleasure in the biologic dimension, for example, you may want to skip that chapter. Or you may want to skim it to make certain you are not lacking a vital piece of information. If lust or desire has always been elusive, you may want to go to the desire dimension in chapter 4 straightaway. Or you may choose to begin with the sensual or the heart dimensions. It is your book and your unique sexual voyage.

However you progress through the book, pay special attention to the sexual tools that come at the end of each chapter and use the ones that appeal to you. These suggestions have been utilized by hundreds of couples as they developed exceptional sexual relationships; they will work for you as well. By practicing these techniques, you and your partner will see immediate results and a renewed positive energy in your sex life.

A multidimensional approach to sex transforms sexual problems and discomforts and gives couples a new source of nourishment for themselves and a deep, inner satisfaction that comes from profound connection with their partner. If your goal is both to love the person you're with and to stay with him or her in a lasting, deeply satisfying physical relationship, then you need the positive energy of each of the seven dimensions.

Sex is powerful. It is a nexus of our physical, emotional, psychological, and spiritual selves. Yet there is a tremendous tension between wanting to believe that wonderful sex is possible and fearing to try—which is either a fear of disappointment or of the unknown. Nevertheless, ecstatic sex is not only possible, it's our birthright. Magnificent sex is what we all deserve; the challenge is claiming that treasure for yourself. As you travel this road, you will undoubtedly learn much about yourself and be changed as a lover, so enjoy the trip to multidimensional, magnificent sex!

2

Sex and the Body

MAKING YOUR BODY FUNCTION
AT ITS SEXUAL PEAK

THE BODY CONNECTION

Sex at its most essential level happens in and through the body, and when we are in touch with our body, it can become the vehicle for immensely satisfying, mind-blowing sex. We know how to prolong sexual pleasure for ourself and our partner. We can count on our body responding to our desire, and we can orgasm when and how we want to. We have both the skill and the control to release sexual tension. We know the map of our lover's body, as well as our own.

The body is where it all begins. We may experience sex in our heads, feel it rush through our emotional center, and yes, even become awash with sex at a spiritual level. But unless the body, the human machine, is functioning in the healthiest way possible, then no amount of mental or soulful desire will let you have great sex.

When you understand how your body works sexually, understand its anatomy and know how it responds sexually, then your overall sexual satisfaction and degree of pleasure will increase. This knowledge leads to a positively energized, optimal biologic dimension. That said, what is optimal for one person may be inadequate or too charged for another person. Our bodies, like ourselves, are all unique, and finding our own way of being in touch with our body is the key to transforming sex at the body level (i.e., the biologic dimension). Yet no matter what shape our body is in or how young or old we are, all of us have the same wonderful potential to find a higher degree of sexual fulfillment. Finally, knowing the common pitfalls of the biological dimension helps us avoid potential or current diminished sexual response. No matter whether our body is in or out of shape, whether we are planning for babies or retirement, or whether we need medications, hormones, or just sleep, I believe all of us have the potential to find a higher degree of physical, sexual fulfillment by focusing on this dimension.

If you'd like to know more about your body, how it functions sexually, and what health, medical, or emotional conditions may be impacting it, then this chapter will provide important, useful information. If your body is in the midst of changing, aging, or recovering from injury or illness, I will help you better understand what is going on. I will share with you case studies and profiles of women and men, as individuals and as couples, who have encountered various obstacles that got in the way of their sexual enjoyment.

Quite simply, if you are in touch with your body, know how to trigger sexual pleasure, then your ability to enjoy sex— from foreplay to orgasm—will increase. All of us have the potential for a strong, passionate connection to our body. You deserve not only the delight of a body humming along sexually, but also the satisfaction of knowing it's functioning at its best.

At its most basic level, sex is a biologic function. And once you see how the body is made to have sex, once you have mastered the sexual facts, you will become your own sex expert. Recently I was conducting a women's sex workshop when a newly married, forty-year-old woman began describing her recent sexual problems. She was happy with her husband, she said, except for one thing. When her husband realized that she was unable to have an orgasm during just straight intercourse, he told her this made him feel that she just must not *really* love him, because otherwise she would be able to let go. Both the woman and her husband had come to me at a crossroads in their sex life. This woman's "problem" was hardly an indication that she didn't love her husband; instead, it showed a gap in his knowledge. Her husband had not been aware that most women cannot experience an orgasm "with just straight intercourse."

Do you know how often I have heard variations of this same story? Many otherwise intelligent women and men do not know enough about their sexual bodies and unwittingly create blocks or obstacles to their own pleasure. These aren't real biological problems; rather, they are consequences that result from a failure to understand how our bodies function sexually.

I have also observed another troubling phenomenon: many women and men, of all ages and backgrounds, are still reluctant to talk about "problems" in bed. Take erections for example. It's usually the woman who first, hesitantly, brings up the subject and describes how her man is either having trouble getting or keeping an erection. When I casually ask if she's talked about this with her lover, nine times out of ten she responds, "Oh, *no*, it would be too embarrassing for him." Now, I ask patiently, how is *not* talking about the obvious going to solve the sexual problems in your relationship?

As the surveys show, thousands of men and women across the country have problems with biologic sexual functioning. If this is you, you are *not* alone. The challenge is to gather the necessary information and take the necessary steps so that you can do everything possible to remedy the situation. Do not allow yourself to fall into the common trap in which you neglect very real physical and biological problems. Over and over again in my practice I encounter well-meaning couples who admit having been reluctant to seek out information or answers to their questions. They often feel stuck, unable to get the advice that would again free them sexually. They want to feel open and spontaneously in touch with their bodies, but something has gotten in the way. They want to be skillful lovers but have not found a way to learn and practice the basics of the game.

Some men and women I've treated describe losing connection to their sexual responses. Some of these people are experiencing the physical effects of aging. Others lose touch with their sexual self because of hormonal or medication effects. Still others claim they have never noticed the physical signs of arousal, experienced an orgasm, or felt the surge of pleasure with ejaculation. They haven't lost the connection: they never had it.

What do you do when, after a few years of passionate sex, one or both of you suddenly struggles to have an orgasm? How can you expect yourself to let go and get into free, abandoned sex if your hormones are out of whack? How can you and your partner discover new ways of pleasuring one another if your recent surgery or medication has taken away your libido, or if you are dealing with the sexual orders of the infertility doctor telling you when and where to have intercourse? In order to have passionate, magnificent sex with a joyous sense of abandon, we need to know what's going on with our body sexually and do our best to see that it is functioning at its peak.

First you need to have reliable, accurate information about anatomy, then you need to become familiar with the amazing sexual response patterns we all have, and finally, you need to become enlightened about what sneaky factors might be interfering with your or your mate's optimal function. With this fundamental information, you will not only begin to feel more in sync with your body and with your partner during sex, you will also feel more comfortable taking the necessary steps when a problem or change crops up. And remember, if you already feel comfortable with how your body works sexually, then you may want to review the checklist at the end of this chapter or simply skip this chapter and go on to the next, where I describe the sensual dimension.

A BRIEF ANATOMY LESSON

One of the most fascinating aspects of becoming a doctor is learning how a human develops from a tiny group of cells. And while I don't expect you to share this enchantment with the science of the body, I do think you may find some of the basic sex differences and similarities between men and women intriguing and insightful. Much of the confusion men and women experience in having sex with each other can be clarified when we understand what sexual equipment we share. Although from the outside women and men look very different, we don't start out that way.

The anatomical blueprint for both sexes is actually the same until testosterone enters the stage. In utero, all human beings start out looking female. But when testosterone appears, the basic female anatomy is transformed into the male genitalia. In fact, if a baby with XY chromosomes, a genetic male, does not produce testosterone in utero, he will be born with female genitalia.

THE OVARIES AND THE TESTICLES

The ovaries in the female and the testicles in the male are the producers of the critical DNA carriers of the genetic data of the human species. In males, what were the ovaries in the female become the testicles, which then make the journey through the inguinal canal down into the scrotum, where they are tethered by their blood, nerve, and sperm channels. Doctors theorize that this descent by the testicles is apparently to seek a cooler temperature for better sperm viability. This is obviously a powerful evolutionary force, because the downside of having your gonads on the outside is that they are much more vulnerable to injury. In fact, every young boy learns that his testicles are sensitive and easily traumatized, producing a nauseating, sick feeling. (In a similar manner, some women also complain of a deep aching and nausea when their ovaries are swollen by a cyst or by the release of the monthly egg.) In females, the ovaries never go anywhere; they stay, snug and secure, in the pelvis.

THE LABIA AND THE SCROTUM

What about the labia majora, those larger lips that surround the vaginal opening in women? These lips seal together in males and become the scrotal sack, which holds the testicles. If you take a nice, close look at the scrotum you can see the seam running down the middle, which marks the fusion of the labia as the male fetus was forming.

Next come the labia minora. They are the thinner, inner lips of the female, which do not have any hair follicles on them. These lips fuse together and form the shaft of the penis in the male. The penis has cylinders of spongy tissue that fill with blood and produce an erection. In a similar manner the labia minora have the same type of tissue that fills with blood during sexual arousal, causing them to swell and stiffen. As they turn outward during arousal, some of the moisture from the vagina coats their surface, making intercourse easier. Mother Nature knew what she was doing!

THE CLITORIS AND THE PENIS

The clitoris is analogous to the tip of the penis. The hood over the clitoris becomes the foreskin in the male. Only a small part of the clitoris is seen externally because the "legs" of this sensitive structure extend inward along the roof of the vagina. The clitoris may be small, but it is mighty. Over 65 percent of women need direct clitoral stimulation for orgasm. This of course makes perfect sense if you realize that it corresponds to the male's sensitive tip. Intercourse is designed for maximum stimulation of this part of the male anatomy—some women wryly comment this proves God must be a man because intercourse usually does not give this same attention to the clitoris, which remains essentially hidden and protected. This anatomical fact means the clitoris needs direct stimulation from his hand, your hand, the pillow, or some other body part for the majority of women who wish to be orgasmic during intercourse. However, the fact that a large part of the clitoris extends along the roof of the vagina leads us to the next interesting anatomical analogy.

THE SACRED SPOT AND THE PROSTATE

The G spot (named after gynecologist Ernst Grafenberg and discovered by Dr. Beverly Whipple) is a sensitive region one to two inches inside the vaginal opening. These researchers have found that this spot clearly responds to stroking by swelling, becoming firmer, and developing a ruffled texture that distinguishes it from the rest of the vagina. Eastern sex manuals call the G spot the "Sacred Spot." If you are a woman, you may already be familiar with this region of your vagina. If not, maybe your partner can help you locate it. Try using a gentle come-hither gesture with one or two fingers and reach to touch the ceiling or roof of the vagina. At first, there may be the feeling of having to urinate or even a slight discomfort. However, with continued gentle stroking (I often tell men to use their nondominant hand) you may begin to feel a deep, tingly sensation. Even if you don't feel an immediate sexual sensation, touching in this area may simply relax you, helping you to open up and connect with your body more intimately.

THE PROSTATE

The prostate gland is deep behind a man's scrotum, where it produces the fluid that carries and nourishes the sperm. The organ can be felt through the rectum, a procedure that most men do not look forward to when the doctor examines the prostate for enlargement or cancer. However, many men do find that massage of the prostate is deeply pleasurable. It's unfortunate that massaging the prostate is often linked to the idea of homosexual sex, preventing many heterosexual men from exploring this sensitive region of their anatomy.

External massage can be accomplished by firmly pressing on the area behind the scrotum but in front of the anus. Men find that circular pressure here is wonderful, especially when coupled with stimulation of the penis, and also useful for prolonging that intense time just before ejaculation.

AROUSE THE BODY

Now that you have a better picture of your sexual anatomy, you may want to understand more about what exactly happens in the sexual act itself. Over thirty-five years ago, Masters and Johnson provided all of us with the basic human sexual response cycle. At that time, they were the first to pinpoint that men and women experience sex in four stages: arousal, plateau, orgasm, and resolution. When you understand this basic cycle, you are in a better position to explore, experiment with, and adjust how you make love with your partner. Part of the challenge of sex is getting in sync with your lover so that you know each other's timing. Having this knowledge helps you to control your body so that you can experience more pleasure. And of course you will become a more skillful lover when you know how to touch your lover in his or her favorite way.

STAGE ONE—LUBRICATION AND ERECTION

In both males and females during the initial phase of sexual arousal, the heartbeat quickens, breathing becomes faster and deeper, and blood flows into the pelvis. And the nipples in both women and men become erect, and the skin becomes warm.

Female Lubrication

When a woman's delicious erogenous zones are stimulated through kissing and touching of her breasts, nipples, vagina, and clitoris, her body will respond by beginning to exude a silky fluid through the walls of the vagina. Lubrication is the first sign of sexual arousal in women. As the blood flows into all the structures of the pelvis, the vagina moistens, and the labia majora and minora begin to swell and become duskier in color.

Physiologically, lubrication is identical to erection in the male, yet women often take much longer to lubricate than men do to get an erection. Why? Because of the pervasive cultural lessons we learned so long ago (and so well): if you allow your sexuality to have freedom of expression, you will get pregnant, a bad reputation, or a disease, perhaps even a lethal one. As a result, women learn to control their sexual urges. No wonder it takes us longer to respond sexually and to connect with our sexual selves that have been buried under years of warnings!

If our bodies are left alone, it will only take seven or eight seconds to lubricate! How many of you have been at the beach with a sexy book, read a chapter or two, and gotten up to take a walk, only to find you're quite lubricated down there! It doesn't take long when there is no fear or demand to perform sexually—our bodies will naturally respond as they were designed to during arousal.

But often women feel their partner is way ahead of them during a sexual encounter. You know how it goes: he has had an erection for five or ten minutes, walking around the bedroom, showing it off, and you have not even begun to lubricate. Who is ahead? He is! If this is your scenario, it is going to take you longer to get to the same level of arousal as your man.

Men, if you want to have your woman matching you on the passion curve, you have to make sure that she is well lubricated before proceeding. The treasure unearthed by the patient partner who understands this difference and gently explores the soft lips, the warm vagina, and the sensitive sacred spot is a beautiful release of energy that blesses him as well. This release may be the first of multiple orgasms, or it may open the lock on a deeper connection that has remained hidden from a hurried lover.

Patience and a loving touch are the most useful tools to problems of lubrication. However, women can at times find themselves dry. This can be caused by medications, such as antihistamines, that dry out body tissues, or by a lack of the hormone estrogen, which is essential for lubrication. You may even feel that you *are* aroused, yet the moisture is not there. In those cases, some useful over-the-counter products include Replens, Lubrin, Gyne-Moistrin, Moist Again, or my favorite for intercourse, Astroglide. I love this name! Undoubtedly it was bestowed by a man who envisioned himself gliding into the warm, wonderful vagina "astrally"!

Erection

An erection is the first stage of a man's arousal. As we learned previously, the dilation of vessels in the pelvis and the genitals fills the spongy cylinders of the penis with blood that is trapped in the shaft and tip. And while some men become erect at the mere sight of their naked lover, other men, no matter the intensity of their desire, have trouble getting or staying erect. Problems with erections worsen with age and can be a huge source of shame for men. One couple I treated are a perfect example of how harmful these feelings of shame can be.

Jim and Susan were a delightful couple from the Midwest who came to see me to discuss their decreasing sexual interaction. Jim had visited his regular physician many times to discuss his trouble with erections and had used injections of testosterone, which had been helpful in the beginning of his difficulties. He had also tried a ring around the base of the penis to try to keep the blood in the shaft, but found it uncomfortable.

After three years of struggling to find a solution to his difficulty keeping an erection, he had begun to avoid sex. His wife, Susan, had also reacted; she no longer felt comfortable initiating any amorous touching or kissing because she did not want to make Jim feel bad.

Jim was uncertain whether he would be able to get an erection or how long he'd be able to keep it. Since he could not control his penis and his performance, he just avoided the whole embarrassing situation.

The Viagra Victory

The solution to Jim and Susan's problem was Viagra. Although doctors had acknowledged erectile dysfunction, or ED, as it is now called, for years, the treatments were cumbersome or downright uncomfortable. Men did not really want to use vacuum devices to pull the blood into the penis and then keep it there with a tight ring around the base. They did not like giving themselves shots into the penis to get an erection or placing a small pellet in the urethra at the tip to be able to function sexually. Can you blame them? The most radical treatment was surgical insertion of a prosthesis that could be pumped up into the shaft of the penis!

All of this changed when Viagra arrived on the evening news, especially with former Republican presidential nominee Bob Dole as Viagra's spokesperson. An oral drug that is taken an hour before an erection is desired, it works by blocking the enzyme that allows the blood to leave the penis. As I often tell men and women who are dealing with this problem, it's a question of plumbing. The blood flows into the penis, but it flows right back out, a condition that increases with age. With Viagra, the flow out is stopped, and the erection is strengthened and preserved.

Some individuals cannot take Viagra, including men who are on nitrates for their heart disease, take multiple medications for serious blood-pressure problems, or suffer from a rare eye disease, retinitis pigmentosa. As with any medication, you need to speak with your doctor before taking Viagra. It is not a good idea to order it over the Internet *or* to take it "just to see" how magnificent your erection can be. It is also important to understand that Viagra is not an aphrodisiac; just because you took it, you will not immediately feel the need to race to bed. Some men experience such side effects as headaches or a slight blue cast to their vision. I always tell patients to start with the lowest dose and to take the minimum required for erection. What do you use the hour for after you have taken the medicine? Sensual pleasure, of course.

Unfortunately, medical pharmacology is still quite unsophisticated in its approach to female sexual response. One unexpected by-product of the Viagra revolution of treatment for male erectile dysfunction is that researchers are now examining whether the same chemistry applies to women who have struggled with arousal and orgasmic difficulties. At this point, Viagra is not a revolutionary drug for women. Some women report improved sexual response, but controlled studies have not demonstrated any consistent response from women, which is too bad. Countless women can become sexually aroused but can never get to the next stage of orgasm. For these women the orgasmic training programs of Lonnie Barbach, Joseph Lopicollo, and Margo Anand (see resource section) are wonderful sources that open up the world of orgasm.

STAGE TWO—THE PLATEAU

The second stage of arousal for women is a subtle, often overlooked part of the whole sexual picture because it happens more internally. This is when the vagina elongates—the uterus having moved up and out of the way—and balloons in the upper third to make room for the penis. This ballooning of a woman's vagina is an inverse of the male erection. For men, the plateau stage is indicated by further swelling of the penis, but otherwise there are no other physiologic changes. However, psychologically and emotionally, the plateau is important because it is here that both men and women need to increase their attention and sensitivity to their bodies. Often in a rush for the climax, we overlook the power and beauty of this waiting period, where deep connection and intimacy can be exquisitely felt. By focusing on the pleasure of arousal, we make ourselves that much more ready for the release of orgasm.

STAGE THREE—THE MYSTERIES AND MAGIC OF ORGASM

As you may imagine, both women and men expend a great deal of mental and physical energy trying to orgasm. An orgasm can be an intense form of pleasure, as well as an intimate way to connect with your partner, but it is also only one of many ways to increase your sexual enjoyment.

Female Orgasms

When I ask women whether they have orgasms, I sometimes get the reply "Well, kind of." The explanation of this hedging answer is usually that the woman can be orgasmic with manual or oral stimulation, but not with intercourse. To this I reply, "Join the club!"

From the strictly physiologic point of view, an orgasm is the contraction of the upper third of the vagina and the uterus every eight-tenths of a second. Some women are well aware of this in their body, while others feel that their mind leaves their body or they see, as I half-teasingly say, "the white light."

Most women say they learned how to have an orgasm either with self-stimulation or with a patient, attentive partner. Women also say that though they become aroused and turned on mentally, they are not able to experience orgasm, which can be extremely frustrating, leading to despair about their sexual performance.

Orgasms are often a relearned response. As infants, we have the ability to orgasm, and ultrasound films have shown fetuses stimulating their genitalia in utero. However, our culture successfully buries this skill in childhood, especially in females, and then countless women feel ashamed or mystified about how to achieve orgasm. One woman in a sexuality workshop said that for years she had told her sexual partners that she was a "broken dolly." She had decided she couldn't have orgasms, and her lover shouldn't even try to produce one in her since she'd never be able to "get there."

Another woman chimed in that her previous husband had ridiculed her for not being easily orgasmic and had said that he really had no choice but to go out and find a "real woman." *Ouch.* Even today, married to a wonderful new husband, her shame kept her from telling him of this previous emotional abuse, and she now feels even more humiliated by her lack of orgasmic responsiveness.

Clearly there are huge differences in orgasmic ease among women. One friend of mine described always being aware of her orgasmic capabilities. In second grade she spent many a recess going up and down the pole on the playground having orgasms, although she did not know at the time what that great feeling was. Me? I was hanging by my knees on the monkey bars unaware of other delights available in the school yard.

Even though women understand that they are not defective or even unusual in requiring direct clitoral stimulation, they may want to develop the ability to orgasm more easily. In many cases, one position may work better for you than others. For example, some women may prefer to be on top with their pelvis rocked forward. Others may need and want some manual touching of the clitoris along with intercourse. Other women prefer intercourse from behind, which allows them to touch their own clitoris while their partner is deep inside. The key to experiencing the deep release and pleasurable sensation of an orgasm is finding the way you like to be touched, caressed, and stimulated. There is no one way; and there certainly is no one right way. I suggest experimenting with different combinations of positions and touches to expand your repertoire.

Other women who have never experienced an orgasm feel that their lack of response is related to never having had the safety of a secure sexual relationship in which to explore how they like to be touched. Still other women feel they are anorgasmic (unable to orgasm) because they have suffered some kind of emotional or sexual abuse. Yet I am certain that some anorgasmia has a physiologic cause that science has yet to understand clearly.

Laura, a woman in one of my pre-orgasmic classes, had never, to her knowledge, experienced an orgasm. Brought up in a strict home where sexuality was never mentioned, she was expected to delay any sexual experimentation until marriage, and she followed that edict. When she finally had intercourse with her new husband, she remembered the first time as somewhat painful and underwhelming. For Laura, marriage and sex two to three times a week was quickly followed by pregnancy and the exhaustion of caring for a new baby. Four other children arrived in close succession, and by the time she came to my group, she despaired of ever being sexually responsive and orgasmic.

Initially, she had to overcome the hesitation of speaking about sexual anatomy and sexual feelings. However, she became intrigued with the functions of the body and, like all good mothers, had dealt with enough body issues with her young and growing children to see that her knowledge of sexual activity needed to be expanded.

Soon, she felt enormous relief and delight in all the information about sexual anatomy and responsiveness, and I advised her to follow a program of self-stimulation to find out information about her own body. Even so, it was with trepidation that she went home to touch herself. Now equipped with massage oil, she turned on some music, and after the relaxation of a warm bath, she tried to become orgasmic. Her goal was to be able to give this information on her technique to her husband, who was eager to help her with the project. Midweek, she excitedly left a message on my answering machine that she had had success with her homework and was delighted by her body's sensations.

The following week at the group meeting, Laura related that after she had had an orgasm, she realized that she had experienced orgasms in the past. She astonished the group by informing us that she had had an orgasm every time she delivered a baby. I was more than a little surprised. I had delivered many babies and had never observed the birth mother orgasmic at actual delivery! Laura went on to become confident of her sexual responsiveness and ultimately was able to show her husband how to touch her. She discovered that she liked slow, light stroking over the tip of her clitoris followed by touches through the hood along the body of the clitoris, and finally the combination of vaginal stroking with direct clitoral touching when she was really aroused. She had to give her husband the additional instruction to change the pressure and speed of touch to avoid "clitoral numbness," but that when she was close to orgasm, she wanted him not to stop or change anything at that moment! Needless to say they both became more skillful lovers with this detailed communication.

Most women believe that an orgasm will literally hit them over the head. I would wager that if you speak to any of your friends, they would tell you the standard line: you'll definitely know when you have one. Yet in Laura's case, she had been orgasmic at least a few times in her life and had not actually known that was what was happening.

Of course, orgasms can be big or small, short or long. When women begin to pay more attention to how and where they feel the arousing stimulation and the tingling sensation of an oncoming orgasm, they become more aware of the subtleties of orgasm. Often their attention to sensual detail, coupled with an increasing ability to let go, makes it easier to be orgasmic. Feeling relaxed and trusting of your partner also helps. You may even want to try letting him watch you touch yourself. Tremendous intimacy can be created by sharing this private moment.

Female Ejaculation

Over my years of sexual counseling, more than a few women have described the release of fluid from their urethra during sex. Early on in my medical career, I thought these women had simply and unfortunately lost control of their bladder sphincter and released some urine. I was wrong. Research has now documented female ejaculation and actually analyzed the fluid that is emitted. The liquid was found to contain a chemical, an acid phosphatase, that is only found in one other gland, the male prostate. This finding implies the existence of vestigial glands along the channel from the bladder, the urethra, that produce fluid for female ejaculation. Many women have found that stimulation of the sacred spot produces this release. Other women bear down as they feel this swelling from increased stimulation in the vagina, which can also produce the ejaculation. Since most women tighten as they approach orgasm, this may be a completely different way to come. Is ejaculation necessary for good sex? No. Is it something to be ashamed of? Absolutely not. Most women who ejaculate explain that it occurs when they feel safe and free with their partner and happens only when they are certain that it will not be viewed with alarm by their lover. If you know you may ejaculate, try putting a towel on the bed. Then, if you want to use massage oil, a vaginal lubricant, or if you ejaculate, you won't have to be thinking about the laundry!

Male Ejaculation

For men in our culture, ejaculation is usually equated with orgasm. However, in other (usually Eastern) cultures, ejaculation is not synonymous with orgasm. For example, in Indian Tantra and Chinese Tao systems, an orgasm is experienced as a flow of energy throughout the body. The man may choose when or even if he wants to ejaculate. The withheld sperm is seen as a way to conserve energy and to reroute it throughout the body for added strength. This is very different from the Western view that withholding ejaculation is bad for your body.

I believe that a man can draw tremendous strength from and control over his orgasm by learning how to control his ejaculation. This enables a man to prolong his pleasure and learn to have multiple orgasms. (Certainly, men, your partner may welcome this too! You have a greater chance of taking her to orgasm, and you can use the energy generated for anything in your life.) This concept is a bit of a hard sell to Western men; however, the control achieved by being able to "play the edge of arousal" and to orgasm throughout the body is a wonderful skill for lovemaking.

Some men find that, as they age, the ability to have an ejaculation wanes in conjunction with difficulties of erection. A man may become so detached during lovemaking, especially if he is overly self-conscious, watching and worrying about his ability to achieve or maintain an erection, that even when he does have a good erection, he may find it difficult to ejaculate. Other men get distracted during sex so that the entire interaction becomes mechanical. If this has happened to you during sex, you may have wondered, "How long is this going to take?" And finally, medications (discussed below) can certainly influence the ability to ejaculate.

Other men suffer from premature ejaculation. Married for twenty-seven years, Sally and Chris came to see me when they had gone without sex for four years. Chris matter-of-factly stated that he had ejaculated prematurely for many years, which always embarrassed him. In fact, because of this, he believed that he would never be able to fully satisfy Sally, reporting that at times she cried after a sexual encounter because she felt so frustrated at the inability to have the release of orgasm. Sally didn't try to hide her anger at what she considered his ineptitude as a lover. He now had trouble even getting an erection, which had consequently made him avoid any sensual or sexual contact.

For Chris and Sally, the emotional pain around sex was great enough that although they planned to continue to live their lives together, they were celibate rather than face the humiliation of sexual failure. By the time they made an appointment with me, they had almost given up hope that anything could help them. The solution for Sally and Chris was to redirect their sexual pattern from failure to success. Without any intention of having intercourse, Chris began to arouse Sally manually. Sally initially felt somewhat guilty about just receiving pleasure, but Chris actually felt more potent than he had in months by being able to give her sexual pleasure. During these sessions, his erections returned as he responded to Sally's lubrication and obvious pleasure. As Sally learned to orgasm with his stimulation of her sacred spot and clitoris, she felt her anger seep away and she became much more interested in helping Chris learn ejaculatory control. She began her own program of stimulation of his body. First she sensually touched his face and upper body. She taught him to tolerate nipple stimulation and overall body pleasure without hurrying to the next stage. Next, he was able to communicate how close he was to coming when she touched his penis rather than keeping his feelings inside as he struggled to control his urges alone. Finally, they carefully began to have intercourse, with many pauses and exquisite communication until Chris could not only tolerate the sensations of a warm, soft vagina but relax into the experience of pleasure knowing he could communicate to Sally where he was on the sexual arousal curve. What had been an antagonistic experience now turned into a pleasure game with both of them on the same team.

STAGE FOUR—RESOLUTION

This stage of the sexual response is when all of the changes you have experienced from increased heart rate to pelvic blood flow return to normal. If there has been an ejaculation, the man has to deal with the refractory period (the rest period when he cannot get another erection or have another ejaculation). For young men, the refractory period can last as little as a few minutes. Older men may even take a day or two to recover, hence the wisdom of considering orgasm without ejaculation as we discussed above. It is also perfectly natural for a man to fall asleep after coming—sometimes a frustrating experience for women. I tell women not to take this personally; this is a physiological response in men, so letting him take a little nap is really okay.

Women, on the other hand, often feel a surge of energy following orgasm. In fact, some women complain to me that they do not want to have orgasms at night because they will be awake for hours afterward. Also women have that wonderful gift of being able to orgasm, rest, and then orgasm again and again. Multiples are not necessary, but they are nice, especially if you have time to experience different types of orgasms, such as ones from G spot stimulation, clitoral touch, or a combination of the two.

BECOME A BIOLOGIC EXPLORER

Now that you are more familiar with the human sexual response, it is time to find out about your partner in detail. Become a sexual investigator: ask, ask, ask your lover questions! How does this feel? Do you like this? Where should I touch you? Is this too much? Would you like me to go slower? Tell me more.

Sometimes we do not even know ourselves what we want, so experiment with one another and become coconspirators in exploring the biological dimension. Imagine that you are going to be continually discovering ways to stimulate your partner and that every couple of weeks you will ask, "What new thing would you like me to do?" We don't ask because we are often afraid of the answer. Perhaps your partner does want a type of sexual activity that may be difficult for you; you can consider it or you can suggest a variation. As you will see in the desire dimension, one of the most common complaints of long-term lovers is boredom; much of this reaction is because we have lost the attitude of the investigator, the explorer. I believe that we allow ourselves to lose our curiosity, our sense of discovery, where our lover is concerned.

This exchange needs to be a two-way street; therefore, you also have to be willing to answer questions, to share your experiences and preferences. Exposing the body, being "investigated," and allowing exploration require trust. This grown-up game of "doctor" is important. It is fundamental to having sexual skill and accurate information about one another. It can also be fun and a wonderful way to increase your intimacy and deepen your love for each other.

1. How does he/she like to be touched?
2. Do you both enjoy oral sex?
3. Do you enjoy letting him come in your mouth? Do you prefer to spit or swallow?
4. Does he have a particular pattern of veins on the shaft? Where is he the most sensitive? What is the stroke that he especially likes you to use? What about his nipples?
5. Where is she most sensitive on her labia? Does she like to be touched with a soft motion or more of a rapid, rubbing motion?
6. Does she like her clitoris touched through the hood or is direct contact okay? How about tapping the clitoris, whispering over it, touching it and the sacred spot at the same time?

Finding techniques to try with your mate is easy. The books listed in the resource section have many suggestions, as do the instructional videos, which have been used by numerous couples in the sexuality workshops as they enhanced their lover's skills.

HOW DO HORMONES AFFECT SEX?

Without our hormones, men and women would be eunuchs or asexual beings. When they are out of balance naturally, or when they are replaced improperly, the body (and the mind) usually knows something is wrong. If they are in the correct proportion, we assume we will have boundless energy, not to mention great sexual performance. If they are bad, we decide they are very bad, causing irritability, bloating, and an undeniable sexual lethargy.

Most of us have been aware of their sneaky influence on our lives since adolescence. We have blamed hormones, encouraged them, and then questioned them. These hormones can be quite fickle: just when you need them the most, they begin to change and you are no longer able to count on them. The main hormones that affect our sexuality are estrogen, testosterone, and progesterone. I have provided below a summary of the importance of these hormones to sexual functioning and indicated what happens sexually when hormones are unbalanced. This is not a complete discussion of hormonal effects throughout the body, but use this information as a guideline to ask yourself if you or your partner has sexual dysfunction due to hormonal imbalance.

THE ROLE OF ESTROGEN

For women, estrogen is a crucial substance. There are three major estrogens in the body: estrone, estriol, and estradiol. Estradiol is the most potent of the three. The major source in women of estradiol is the follicle or egg sack of the ovary. When these follicles are depleted at menopause, or when the ovaries are surgically removed or their function destroyed by chemotherapy or radiation, women report dramatic changes in their sexual functioning.

Betty came to me out of desperation. She had heard that I treated individuals with sexual problems. Betty complained of dyspareunia, pain with intercourse. Had she always had pain? No, her pain had started with menopause. Before then, she and her husband had made love about twice a week without any discomfort on her part. Now her vagina was so dry, she cringed at the thought of sex. None of the lubricants they had tried seemed to last long enough, and even if there was enough moisture, she still felt sore the next day. On a couple of occasions she had even bled from the raw areas.

In Betty's case I made a simple diagnosis. A serum estradiol test revealed that Betty had almost no estrogen in her bloodstream. I put Betty on an estrogen patch, in which she received the hormone through her skin. Within days her vagina felt better, and within weeks sex again became a pleasant experience rather than an ordeal.

As I have noted above, many vaginal lubricants are available, with estrogen vaginal creams as well as oral doses or dermal patches available for supplement. A new form of replacement estrogen is a silicone ring, which resembles a diaphragm, with a small amount of estrogen. The ring contains the equivalent of two days' worth of an oral dosage that is then gradually released over three months. This ring can even stay in place in the vagina during intercourse and releases estrogen only to the local tissue, avoiding a systemic rise in blood levels of estrogen. Many women who are leery of taking estrogen or who have medical contraindications find this a great alternative to messy vaginal estrogen creams.

Although there is still great confusion and debate about whether to take estrogen, most women understand that it is a risk/benefit calculation that each person has to make. In addition, women are increasingly aware of the variety of preparations that are now available. I do a tremendous amount of counseling about hormone replacement therapy and the types of therapy available, including the natural sources of estrogen and progesterone. Each woman who decides to use patches, pills, or creams deserves an individualized approach. Daily we are receiving new data about estrogen, its change in blood levels with alcohol ingestion, its role in possibly preventing Alzheimer's disease, its production by the fat cells of the body. What has yet to be clarified is the clinical significance of these observations. That will be the task of the next decade. Until then, many women will use their sexual comfort as part of the equation in deciding whether to use estrogen. Health care providers are going to be called on to individualize treatment for women according to their unique complaints and responses to therapeutic options. It is about time!

THE IMPORTANCE OF TESTOSTERONE

Testosterone has been called the hormone of desire, fueling our lust and sexual drive—without it we just do not care very much about "doing it." The presence of testosterone is not only linked to sexual desire but also to feelings of well-being and a sense of energy in men and women.

Testosterone and Men

When testosterone levels are high or adequate, men feel alive, vigorous, and sexually tuned in and frequently turned on.

However, testosterone, which is produced by the testicles, decreases gradually and variably with age. At low levels, not only can the male experience diminished libido, but also difficulty attaining an erection. Of course, this is not the sole cause, or even the most frequent reason, for loss of erections (remember, this is usually a "plumbing" problem), but measuring levels of testosterone in the blood or saliva is important as part of the investigation of erectile problems. There are now forms of testosterone replacement using skin patches for men much like estrogen patches for women. Initially, these patches had to be placed on the shaved scrotum for adequate absorption! However, there are now patches, creams, and gels for application to the hairless parts of the skin such as the back, abdomen, or buttocks. All of these preparations are used because testosterone is not readily absorbed from the stomach in pill form, and they have gone a long way in replacing the testosterone injections.

Replacement of testosterone requires a careful analysis of the libido and/or the erectile problem. Because testosterone can stimulate prostatic growth, an evaluation of the size of the prostate as well as measurement of the PSA, prostatic-specific antigen, is required before this hormone is given to men. Another concern is the correlation of testosterone with levels of cholesterol in the blood. If total cholesterol and LDL cholesterol, the "bad" lipid, are high, close follow-up of these blood values is prudent during a trial of the medication. In addition, liver function tests are also checked during treatment.

Women and Testosterone

Yes, women have testosterone as well as men. The ovaries produce about one-third to one-half of this while the adrenal glands account for the rest. The amount of testosterone varies from woman to woman, and production decreases as women enter menopause. When women lose this hormone, they experience not only loss of sexual desire, but also decreased sexual responsiveness. They complain of clitoral numbness, atrophy, and difficulty being orgasmic. It is little wonder that sex is less and less appealing.

This testosterone transition can begin before the loss of estrogen. In this case, the individual may not even consider that she is menopausal because she is still menstruating, and she is not having hot flashes or sleep disturbance. She is at a loss to explain why she has abruptly lost her sexual drive and responsiveness. Of course, many other life changes may be complicating her situation, but a simple blood or saliva test can be extremely helpful in searching for testosterone deficiency.

A huge, neglected group of women with hormonal lack of desire are women who have had an oophorectomy (removal of the ovaries). When the ovaries are removed, usually along with the entire uterus, most gynecologists are alert to the symptoms of estrogen lack. Often, an estrogen patch is placed on the patient in the recovery room to ease the transition from having functioning ovaries to nothing. However, equally as often, testosterone deficiency is ignored. Debra, a thirty-something woman who attended a workshop, told me she had no sexual urges anymore. She rarely was orgasmic and only engaged in sex now because her husband became hurt and irritable if she didn't. I asked her if it was always this way and she said, "Oh, no. I used to really like sex. My husband and I got it on almost every other day."

When did the change occur? Well, when she had had her hysterectomy.

Did the doctors also remove her ovaries? You bet.

Did they check her testosterone when she shyly complained of the loss of sexual urges? Nope.

It was her husband who finally made the correlation. He bitterly observed that no one had warned them that loss of their sex life might be a consequence of her "female surgery." They had argued more than once about whether this operation should have been performed.

Fortunately, the blood test of an extremely low level of free testosterone (the unbound, active form) came back within a few days of her attending the workshop and allowed immediate treatment. Unfortunately, this treatment was begun twelve years after the surgery! During these twelve years, no doctor had taken this patient's complaints seriously, preferring to assume, among other things, that she didn't want sex because she could no longer get pregnant! I could certainly sympathize with her eventual decision not to bring this issue up again—that is, until she joined a sexual enhancement class.

Lest we all run out immediately and insist that our doctors prescribe testosterone, remember that some women continue to make plenty of this hormone despite the loss of ovarian production. Some individuals have sufficient levels because of adrenal sources. And some women with low levels feel fine. Not every midlife or menopausal woman needs this hormone. Also, there can be side effects to reckon with, such as acne, edgy mood, facial-hair growth, or blood cholesterol changes. Usually, these side effects are not seen at low levels of replacement, but they must be watched for as treatment is initiated. Replacement doses can and should be individualized to fine-tune the regimen for an optimal sense of well-being, lean muscle mass, and libido.

As more midlife women are viewed as capable of and, indeed, insistent upon a vigorous lifestyle that includes continued sexual desire and responsiveness, testosterone replacement will become more commonplace as well as sophisticated. A testosterone patch for women is currently being tested. We can all look forward to a future where women will no longer face blank stares as they discuss libido and vitality with their health care providers.

THE POWER OF PROGESTERONE

Progesterone is in many ways a counterbalance to estrogen. Progesterone is produced in a woman's ovary by the egg sac that is left behind after a ripened egg has erupted at ovulation each month. Progesterone prepares the uterine lining for the fertilized egg that nature hopes for. In fact, without sufficient progesterone, even the most perfectly dividing, fertilized egg will have no place to implant after its trip down the fallopian tube from the ovary. Lack of progesterone is therefore one of the causes of infertility.

On the other hand, if there is no fertilization, the progesterone production is quickly exhausted. When the level of progesterone falls, the nicely prepared lining of the uterus begins to separate and is shed as a woman's monthly period. This is all well and good. However, progesterone/estrogen imbalance can wreak havoc with other body systems, producing the notorious PMS, or premenstrual syndrome, as well as breast tenderness, bloating, and irritability.

What does all of this have to do with sex? Well, when your breasts are swollen and weighty, when you have had a headache for two days straight, when irritability is your middle name, you *do not* want to make love. One solution to the estrogen/progesterone teeter-totter is to add some additional estrogen when progesterone is on board. The perimenopausal woman who is still having periods but making less estrogen than she used to may be able to use a low-dose estrogen patch the week before she bleeds to balance the progesterone when it is at its highest. The woman who is menopausal and on a prescribed cycle can increase her dose of estrogen by half again during the days she is taking the progesterone.

Whatever the reasons for the loss of a sense of vitality, hormonal imbalance or not, there is almost always a concomitant decline in sexuality. If you are currently taking hormonal replacement therapy or feel any of your symptoms may be hormonally related, then I recommend a thorough evaluation of the physical aspects of sexual functioning. Hormonal replacement takes fine-tuning for most women. As medicine learns more about both male and female sexuality, as better treatments become available, and as continued vigorous sexual functioning becomes the expectation, this physiologic dimension will be the foundation to the sensual and desire dimensions.

MEDICATIONS THAT IMPACT SEXUAL FUNCTIONING

The list of drugs that adversely affect sexual functioning is huge. Almost all medications have at one time been reported to cause sexual difficulty. So, if you were doing fine until you started a new drug, be sure to ask your health care provider if this drug has a history of similar problems and/or see if another drug is available for the problem. A more complete list of drugs that can affect sexuality is in the resource section, but here are some of the more notorious prescription medications that you may want to watch out for:

▶ Blood pressure medications, especially the beta-blockers such as Atenolol

▶ Antidepressants, especially the SSRIs such as Prozac, Paxil, and Zoloft, but almost all of the antidepressants can be problematic

▶ Cholesterol-lowering meds such as the statins Zocor, Lipitor, and Mevacor or niacin

Diabetes interferes with the microvascular system of the sexual organs as well as the nerve supply and needs to be treated aggressively to avoid long-term sexual consequences. Medication in this case may be an important preventative step.

THE LURE OF STIMULANTS

At one time or another, most of us enjoy sipping a glass of wine or bubbly champagne to get us in the mood, and while a glass of wine or a beer can help relax us, when we regularly rely on mind-altering substances to feel sexual, we are actually numbing our sensuality. The drugs and alcohol dull sensation in the body over time. Alcohol, as we know, is a depressant. It diminishes our response time and judgment, it often puts us to sleep, and it is habituating. It's not so unusual for couples to have a drink or two before dinner, have wine with dinner, and then have an after-dinner drink. All of this drinking is part of their romantic night on the town. But how can they expect to go home and make love after so much alcohol? What do they do? Fall asleep! As Shakespeare said, "Alcohol increaseth the desire but taketh away the performance." In addition, it limits our awareness of the sensory delights that await us during loving with all of our senses awakened and in tune.

My advice: Everything is fine in moderation. You and your partner are the best judge of when outside sources of erotic stimulation or substances are enhancing your sensual experience or distracting you from feeling your sexual connection completely.

STRENGTHENING AND ENERGIZING THE SEXUAL HEALTH OF YOUR BODY

Take action! Having a strong biologic dimension is important, and you owe it to yourself and your lover to make certain this fundamental aspect of sexuality is healthy.

You don't want to begin or continue to neglect any physical problem interrupting or preventing sexual functioning. Many of us feel trapped by our biology, as if we can do nothing about the hand nature has dealt us. But there are approaches to help the woman in menopause, the man with erectile problems, the couple adjusting to the schedule of infertility treatments or a partner's recent surgery. Much of what can destroy this dimension is ignorance and the embarrassment of discussing sex with our doctor. Some of it is the lack of good information available, even from doctors. But please believe that there are many solutions to your problems, and that neglecting the remedies will only increase your frustration and sexual disappointment.

BIOLOGIC DIMENSION CHECKLIST

1. GET THE KNOWLEDGE

First of all, educate yourself. Many books provide programs for becoming orgasmic and techniques to delight your partner and yourself. Numerous tasteful videos illustrate useful techniques to those of us who feel inexperienced. The great thing about videos is how they convey visually the connection between lovers who have as their major goal the sensual pleasuring of their partner, something we will discuss in the sensual dimension. No matter how long you have been having sex, there is always more to learn, so be sure to check out the references in the resource section. I have put my favorites first on the list.

2. GET THE EXPERT OPINION

Ask your physician questions about sexual functioning and look for individuals who have been trained in human sexuality. One great source for information about sex and for referrals in your area is SIECUS, the Sexuality Information and Education Council of the United States. They have a

Web site that can be accessed for sexuality information, and they have staff who answer requests for information. Many of their publications contain pertinent information for adults, even though part of their effort is directed toward education of young people about sexuality. Their address and Web site are listed in the resource section.

3. IMPROVE YOUR BODY

Start to condition yourself physically by increasing the flexibility and strength in your hips, knees, and pelvis. Exercise those PC (pubococcygeal) muscles. Those are the muscles that connect the pubic bone in front with the coccyx, or the tailbone, in back. Woman tighten the vagina and the bladder with these, but they are also important for men as they work to control that ejaculatory urge. You are supposed to do a hundred PC contractions a day! I think they are perfect to do in boring meetings or during endless conference calls. Lovemaking is more fun when you have strength in your legs, a limber body, and a well-conditioned set of genital muscles.

4. LEARN A NEW SEXUAL SKILL

Try becoming multiorgasmic. Map your partner's or your arousal levels so that you always know where each of you is on the sexual response curve. Be willing to try something different physically to stimulate your lover. Women should take steps to ensure proper lubrication. Men should learn techniques to strengthen their erection to increase duration and frequency.

5. CHECK OUT THE HORMONES

If you are using birth control, examine how these hormones affect your sexual response. The new combinations have either more or less androgen (testosterone-like) effects and you may need more for libido or less to curb irritability. If you are hitting midlife, get your hormones tested, especially the active, free testosterone, then decide if you want to consider replacement.

6. TAKE A LOOK AT YOUR MEDS

If you are taking prescriptions, ask your doctor if they could interfere with your sexual functioning. If you suspect diminished response or desire, another drug may work equally as well. Find a physician who is willing to talk to you about sex and who considers it an essential part of being alive.

BODY POWER

Thankfully, just as we are hardwired for sensual input and programmed for procreation, our body is exquisitely designed for sexual responsiveness. The sensual, desire, and biologic dimensions work closely together primarily because we are animals. There is something beautiful and compelling in making love with a fully functioning body. The body is a wonderful source of sexual pleasure, but it needs to be cared for, paid attention to, and honored. Knowledge about the body and its sexual functioning is the key to getting in touch with this physical spirit. So, as we move on to the sensual and desire dimensions, we will further strengthen our physical connection to sex by making our body more in balance, sensually alive and sexually energized. We all deserve sexual body power at its peak!

3

Increase Your Sexual Pleasure Through a Vital Sensual Dimension

Kiss by kiss I travel your little infinity,
your borders, your rivers, your tiny villages;
and a genital fire—transformed, delicious—

—PABLO NERUDA

A RENAISSANCE OF SENSES

On the first really warm day of spring, I find myself going to my closet and putting on my favorite spring dress, soft and flowing around my bare legs. I step outside into the wonderfully fragrant air, listen to the cacophony of birdsongs, and revel in the piercing green of new grass and leaves. I feel the magic around me, and a renewed sense of life, of hope, of inspiration, courses through me.

Nothing has really changed in my life: I still have the same, all-consuming workload, the financial hassles, the nagging worries, but with the turn to warmer weather, these issues suddenly recede as the intoxication of my senses takes over my awareness. I feel invigorated and pleased to be alive. Pleasure is humming through my body.

I am not alone in my response to the headiness of spring.

What is it about this season that allows a sudden renaissance of our senses? Is it some sort of evolutionary response, a throwback to the days when winter meant hibernation and a virtual shutting down and covering up of the body? Perhaps. But for me, the significance of this powerful response to spring is a very natural desire for the sensual, the desire for pleasure.

How do you experience pleasure? Specifically, how do you experience sexual pleasure? Is it tied strictly to the release of orgasm? Or do you feel pleasure more intensely when your lover weaves his fingers through your hair, rubs your shoulders at the end of the day, or takes you on a walk by the sea? Do you feel pleasure more consciously when you are cuddled in your bedroom or when you are on a hike, breathing in fresh mountain air? Do you prefer a slow buildup, in which you prolong foreplay as you and your lover touch, caress, and kiss each other? Or do you like to go straight for the thrill of orgasm, riding that wave as it unfurls in a rush? We all have different styles and approaches to how we get there, but I've learned that the women and men who get the most out of sex (in all its stages) are those who open themselves fully to their sensuality.

I *know* our bodies are biologically "hardwired" for sensuality. As infants, we instinctively seek out the mother's nipple, as much for the skin-to-skin contact that reassures us that we are alive as for the milk. Unable to speak, infants rely on sound, sight, touch, and smell to learn about their world and communicate their needs. Many of us may remember the studies done in the 1960s on baby monkeys, showing that infant monkeys would respond much more positively to a cloth-covered simulated mother than one in which the wires were exposed. The monkeys would drink much more milk from the softer "mother" and seemed afraid and reluctant to snuggle up to the wire-bound "mother." These experiments also demonstrated that when infants (monkeys and humans) are not given any kind of warmth, live touch, interaction, or stimulation, they can actually die. Eventually, these studies became the basis for the theory of maternal deprivation: without human touch, human infants will not thrive. These studies underscore both the primal nature of our senses, especially touch, and their importance to our health and well-being.

The importance of our senses is profound. Before humans existed in a socialized, industrial age, they depended for their survival on their hearing, smell, and sight: these senses provided information to protect them against approaching threats. Now, of course, we don't have to rely on these senses as survival mechanisms in our daily lives. But we still need them to experience our world, and when we get cut off from our senses, this experience becomes foreshortened, hollow. Without our senses to awaken and *enliven* us, we feel numb. Too often we think about our world rather than actually engage in it through our senses. It is as if we have become gigantic heads walking around on teeny, tiny bodies, evaluating, judging, thinking. In a world that mentally assaults us with information at an ever-faster pace, the sensual gets forgotten. Without conscious effort, this dimension can become anemic, starved for sustenance, and results in sensory numbness. This is the most common problem I see with busy, overcommitted partners. But at the negative end of the sensual continuum there is actual pain, emotional or physical, which has to be relieved for this aspect of sex to reach its full potential.

The pleasure of life comes primarily in the experience of life. To have pleasure we must remove the plastic, see-through shield that stands between us and our experience of the world. And when it comes to sex, to feel the tingly, wondrous thrills of our sexuality, we have to open and ignite our own and our partner's sensuality.

And it is this sensuality that feeds our sexuality. When our sensuality is opened and heightened, then we feel sexual pleasure more intensely. How, outside of that first warm day of spring, do we access this kind of tangible pleasure anytime, anywhere? The answer is in the awakening of our senses. When our senses are awakened, we feel more vital, more in tune with our sexual desire, and therefore we are more conscious of physical pleasure.

Most of us assume we have just five senses—sight, hearing, taste, touch, and smell. It is easy to see how they are involved in sex. But I include a sixth, "special" sense of the kinesthetic, which is knowing how to move our bodies. This sense is important in lovemaking because the more aware we are, the more erotic and exciting our sexual connection.

Here's another way to see the power of the senses. A woman who is blind is hardly cut off from sensual experience. Indeed, people who lose one sense generally develop more acute strengths in other senses. So though we can focus on individual senses, the goal in terms of energizing the sensual dimension of our sexuality is to arouse and stimulate the entire body. In the chapter on biologic dimension you learned the importance of knowing and understanding the essentials about sexual functioning so that you can tell whether your body is responding at its sexual peak. In this chapter on the sensual dimension, you will learn how to connect or reconnect with your body so that the energy flows in you, through you, and toward your lover. When the sensual channels are open, sexual pleasure is that much more intense and charged.

When we are sensually awakened, even if we don't have a lover, we feel rewarded and pleased by our own body. Becoming a more sensual creature takes time and focus, but there is tremendous pleasure in feeling your body brimming with energy. After all, sex is the perfect vehicle for intense sensual pleasure.

A vigorous, awakened sensual dimension looks like this:

▶ You have spontaneous, frequent, physical nonsexual contact with your lover or partner, including touching, massaging, dancing, holding, or stretching each other.

▶ You create an atmosphere of sensuality. For example, with such details as scented candles, music, flowers, or lighting, you create an oasis that encourages relaxation and awareness—a condition for the opening of the senses.

▶ You pay attention to nature and/or art. Admire the panorama or a painting, twittering birds or music, lying upon a grassy meadow, or feeling a sculptural curve. This kind of stimulation awakens the senses, paving the way to using these skills during sex.

▶ You practice body awareness by valuing your body enough to condition it. You consume healthy, sensual food, rest when you need to, and have rituals in taking care of your skin and hair that provide ongoing sensual experiences.

In my experience with couples, one partner is usually the sensual leader of the two. She or he has learned to value sensuality in life and is more comfortable and natural opening up to sensuality. This person brings a great gift to the relationship. If your partner is that person, he or she deserves recognition, kudos, for bringing the sensual to your sex. If you are the sensual expert, stand firm in the knowledge that your skill is fundamental to a complete sexual relationship.

The sensual dimension is about increasing our ability to give and receive pleasure and letting it build and move throughout the body. In this chapter, you will see how to revitalize the sensual dimension of your relationship. If you are blocked or numbed, you will see how to unleash this vital energy source. If you experience an even more extreme disruption of this dimension, then you will feel pain, *emotional or physical,* blocking this vital sexual channel. The good news is that these conditions can be healed and strengthened: everyone can have a vital sensual dimension!

OPEN YOUR SENSUAL DOOR

The more you sensually connect with your own body, the more you can extend that sensuality to your partner. Taking time to lovingly apply lotion to your skin after a shower, dancing to the new salsa CD you just bought, feeling the sun on your face as you listen to the birds in the park—all of these activities awaken the sensual. Allowing sexual self-pleasuring, which often arises out of a sensual experience, can be important for developing awareness of what exactly is pleasurable for you. Touching your soft inner lips in the shower or when you are lazily waking up, finding what type of stimulation takes you to the peak of orgasm, exploring the sensitive secrets of your body in private, can open the doorway to a new sensual garden. In time you can invite your lover into this garden, but it is often wonderful to begin discovering its delights on your own. So many of us, however, hesitate to do this.

Does this credo sound familiar: It must be bad if it feels so good? This is an age-old dictum instructing us, even as the smallest of children, not to touch ourselves. So often in our culture, we are told not to enjoy simply pleasuring our bodies. Even today, there is a cultural association between sensual feelings and sinful temptations. Take the example of Diane, now a grown woman of more than fifty years, who came to see me to discuss how hormones were affecting her body. She felt some of the changes that most women do as she lost her estrogen, including mild sleep disturbance, night sweats, and vaginal dryness. As we discussed these symptoms and their effect on her sexuality, she also told me that she had always felt disconnected from her erotic self. Curious, I asked her what she meant by her "erotic self." She replied that she thought she had always been a sensual being, but as a young girl going to a Catholic school, she remembered being alarmed by the strict rules about clothes and especially nakedness. Not only were patent leather shoes out of the question (someone might be able to see up her dress in the reflection!), the nuns in her boarding school would actually powder the surface of the bathwater so that the girls could not even see their own genitals. Of course, as an inquisitive child, this rule made Diane even more interested to see what was down there. She then described to me a vivid memory of being caught with a mirror as she was peeking between her legs to find out what was so private about her body that even she was not allowed to see it.

Diane can now tell this story with a great deal of humor, being distant from her eventual punishment. However, this kind of negative association with our bodies is extremely prevalent. How many of you had your hands slapped for touching yourself as a toddler or were embarrassed or humiliated if you were found pleasuring yourself in your bedroom? Many young men caught masturbating by their father or mother are made to feel as if they have committed a sinful act by exploring their sensual/sexual feelings. The "pleasure police" may actually have existed as authority figures in our lives at some point, but we quickly internalize this law enforcement agency. If, as adults, we don't check for their existence and then banish them to the land of the powerless, they may continue to sound the sirens of shame when we begin to experience sensual gratification, no matter what age we are.

It is important to recognize where the feelings of anxiety began when we engage sensually with our own or our lover's body. An examination of the old "rules" we were raised with allows us to decide whether these rules serve us now as adults. If they do not, as often is the case, we can consciously begin to confront the disabling beliefs that create a barren connection without sensual pleasure. What a relief to finally banish the pleasure police!

An essential part of becoming a sensual being is learning how to receive as well as to give. This sounds easier than it is. You may love to pleasure your partner by giving him or her a massage, back rub, or foot rub. You may eagerly and regularly touch your lover with affection. But are *you* open to being touched? This is often a problem with men and women who feel ashamed of their body. Allowing your partner to pleasure you requires vulnerability, a belief that you deserve to be pleasured, and a willingness to receive pleasure from someone else. Receiving means relinquishing control. That is a scary thought for most of us!

Pamela was an accountant with a strong desire to be in control, always. She came to see me soon after a two-year relationship with a married man had ended. She told me that she realized that she had a pattern of picking men who were unavailable to her because she believed she was not really able to be in a long-lasting passionate relationship. After all, she was an accountant, she explained, and was unable to loosen up enough to be in a relationship. Then she admitted to believing that her body was primarily a vehicle to provide fuel and transportation for her mind.

Bingo! I saw clearly that she had no relationship to her own body and its potential to give her sensual pleasure. In fact, she usually ignored her body and had only recently become more aware of it because she had decided to lose weight. She had lost thirty pounds and was noticing her body (and being noticed) as never before. After evaluating her strengths and weaknesses in the seven dimensions, Pam embarked on a program to become more sensual, incorporating many of the tools described below. It became clear that though she felt desire and knew a lot about her body, she was blocking the sensual energy, and this made her feel unable to participate in a long-term relationship. By learning to let go, she began to develop her confidence as a sexual, sensual woman.

We can all bring more sensuality into our lives and especially into our lovemaking by exploring rather than restricting our connection to the sensual. However, sometimes this means overcoming complicated obstacles from our past.

LIVING IN YOUR HEAD

If sensuality is as natural a state as cuddling a baby or rubbing your lover's back, then how do we lose our connection to the sensual? If sexual arousal (such as erections and lubrication of the vagina) has been noted in babies, why do we stop getting aroused? What happens to those natural sources of energy and pleasure? They go underground, and in their place, numbness or pain takes root.

Numbness comes from extreme detachment from our sensual feelings. This kind of detachment is often found in men and women who have busy mental lives and rely too much on feedback from their brain rather than from their body. Refusing to engage the senses, they stay in their head, ignoring their body. The mind is one busy executive. It is quite happy to be in total control, running the show. It delights in mental sparring and loves to win verbal contests.

Pat and Mike were great at this verbal game. Both lawyers, they were adept at pointing out each other's errors in thinking, opinions, and judgments. One would tell you where they met, and the other would correct the first. They were locked in battles over trivial remembrances of their life together, and each was determined to prevail. By the time they came to see me, their sex life was almost nonexistent, and the concept of pleasuring each other sensually had become a distant memory; they were too busy competing with each other to stop and offer a caress.

At my office, they had barely sat down when they began what I assumed was yet one more battle in their ongoing war of words. Although they seemed unable to agree on a single subject, they insisted that they respected and loved one another and wanted to continue their marriage.

I began asking them about their sexual relationship. They admitted that sex for them was either avoided or an exercise they "just got through," not one filled with passion or pleasure. After listening to them for a couple of sessions, I suggested they try an exercise in which they had to stop talking! I wanted them to start touching, communicating with each other through their hands and eyes, rather than through words. Finally forced to disengage from their intellectual sparring (my guess was that this verbal warfare had begun long ago as a response to discomfort with communicating nonverbally), Pat and especially Mike began to pay attention to the sensual input, which had previously been ignored.

I asked them to try making love in silence, using no words to express their feelings. The challenge was to come toward one another with their senses—a smile, a touch, a kiss—not with their intellects. For Pat and Mike this was truly difficult. The reward, however, was to reclaim their sensual selves, which had long ago been lost in the intensive training of law school and in legal careers.

This simple assignment changed everything because they were in new territory; they had to pay attention to such sensory details as a glance, the quality of touch, a sigh, a moan, the way she or he moved when genitally stimulated. The numbness both felt dissolved and they became excited about learning this new way of communicating. They were determined to win, which meant pulling this dimension from the doldrums of numbness. Not only did their sexual life find new zest, they each felt much more alive in their usual day-to-day activities. There was no going back; they were hooked on the multitude of sensual pleasures life presents us, and they began to take great joy in delighting each other.

WHEN "JUST DOING IT" IS NOT ENOUGH

Everyone has the capacity to connect to sensuality, but some women and men become so detached from their feelings that a simple "just do it" is not enough. Many of these people in my practice who describe themselves as numb to or lacking in sensuality are blocked emotionally. Afraid that sex will lead to their being hurt, they block the arteries to their sensuality, and they no longer feel connected to it. The body has literally shut itself off from experiencing the pleasure. The circulation of sensuality and sexuality is halted by old memories or unnamed fears. In some cases, these people have experienced emotional, physical, or sexual trauma that has directly interfered with their ability to feel pleasure. If, in the case of abuse, the trauma has stretched over many years, a person may even experience pain with sensual arousal and therefore go out of his or her way to avoid sensual and sexual contact.

THE BODY KNOWS

Sometimes you can become disconnected from your sensuality because your body is literally blocking any physical feeling. If you are experiencing physical pain in one part of your body, your sensory channels throughout your body will shut down. As we saw in the biologic dimension, any pain in your pelvic or genital region can impact sexual experience. However, it's also true that if you have pain in any area of your body—your neck, lower back, even your feet—you may not be able to feel other sensual pleasure. The pain may be a result from surgery or certain hormonal changes in menopause. Regardless, I often hear complaints of pain caused by sexual activity. In women, tightness of the vaginal opening has its own label as a sexual dysfunction, vaginismus. Deep pelvic pain may inhibit sexual responsiveness either from uterine or ovarian pathology, or from awkward positions or lack of sufficient arousal during sex. Men sometimes complain of a burning sensation when they ejaculate or pain in the testicles or around the anal opening at or shortly after ejaculation. However, some individuals purposely seek pain as part of their sexual experience. For these men and women who enjoy sadomasochistic sexual encounters, the pain of bondage, piercing, or cutting, for example, can actually heighten their sexual arousal. But for most people, pain decreases sexual arousal and prevents them from feeling sensual pleasure.

My first case as a sexual therapist occurred in medical school during an advanced class that I had organized with a professor who taught human sexuality. Philip Sarrel and his wife, Lorna, were members of the Yale faculty, she a sociologist and he a professor of ob-gyn. I was impressed with the wonderful way they taught human sexuality. At this point in my training, I knew little in terms of the basic physiology of sexuality, and I saw this advanced class as an opportunity to do cotherapy with two highly regarded experts.

One of my first cases in which I was cotherapist was a young couple who had been married approximately one year. I was amazed to find out that they had never had intercourse. The problem? She found it impossible to have intercourse because of pain around the opening to the vagina. After taking a careful history, we scheduled a physical examination of her genitalia to try to understand what was wrong. She related prior to this exam that she had been to other doctors who said the opening was "too tight" and that they would be happy to "cut it open." Thankfully both she and her new husband did not think that was a good response to this problem.

I remember that pelvic exam as if it were yesterday. This brave young woman was seated on the exam table, the back of which had been raised so that she could more easily participate. Her heels were in stirrups and she was draped with a sheet across her legs. I was to conduct the physical examination and, at this point in my training, did not feel entirely competent in doing so but knew that Dr. Sarrel was an ob-gyn with tremendous experience. What I did feel was compassion and an acute sense of this young woman's courage, being in an examining room with two doctors and her husband, exposed and vulnerable. It was a testimony to her desire to come to terms with this problem and also to their mutual desire for her to become pregnant that she went through with the examination.

Soon we discovered that although her external genitalia were normal in every way, we could not examine her vagina because of the spasming of the muscles at the opening. In fact, one could not even put a Q-tip swab into her vagina! Obviously there was no way that her husband was going to place his penis inside the vagina without literally raping her.

Later, as we began to explore the reasons for this intense fear and apprehension, she related her trauma at seeing a movie that depicted a young woman repeatedly raped. She found herself identifying with this young woman to the extent that she became extremely fearful about any genital contact and especially intercourse.

Over the next several weeks, she began to use a set of vaginal dilators, returning one dilator after another until she was able to use by herself a dilator that was comparable in size to a normal penis. In fact, her husband was at times able to help her put in the dilators, and she was able to leave them in for a while to get used to the sensation.

One week the couple came back after having used the largest dilator, and as I walked into the room to do our usual counseling, they were both sitting there literally grinning from ear to ear. I couldn't help but smile back and said, "What's up?" She replied that they had, against the rules, gone ahead and had intercourse during the past week.

"Well, how did it go?" I asked.

"Fine," she said, smiling. In fact, it had been a loving and tender encounter, and she had not had any fear, and most notably, she had not had any pain. Her husband agreed and was delighted that they had finally been able to consummate their marriage. A wonderful transition had taken place. Sex had gone from pain to pleasure with a slow, loving approach—and she had experienced no discomfort! An even more remarkable postscript to this story is that this young couple became pregnant at that first intercourse—fulfilling one of the desires that had brought them to us in the first place.

This was one of the easiest cases of sexual dysfunction I have ever treated and certainly one of the most satisfying. Because of this experience and others, I have continued to work with couples regarding sexuality throughout my medical career. This young woman was a vivid example of someone who had completely closed down her physical and sensual self, such that she had no pleasurable experience during touch or during sexual stimulation.

In many cases, if you have had a painful physical operation or problem, you may shut down right then and there, causing a post-traumatic stress response in the sexual arena, but one that you are unaware of. In these cases, we have to be sexual sleuths to uncover the pertinent history, and then enlighten ourselves so that we can banish the shadow of the experience on our sexual pleasure.

Cindy and Stewart did not really have a good explanation for why they did not make love. They had been married for over twenty-five years and now rarely had sex. Despite their virtual celibacy, they both thought that their marriage was good. Stewart remembered that he had withdrawn from initiating sex when Cindy had told him that their sexual encounters weren't very good. For a long time she had been detached sexually, just going through the motions, and was not experiencing any pleasure with genital touch. Cindy was aware of the numbness she felt during sex and admitted to blaming Stewart for not being a great lover, but she also knew that she had not always been so detached. Stewart withdrew sexually as well and reported that he diverted his attention away from sex by dreaming up more ways to add to his already successful company.

Together and individually, Cindy and Stewart began to look at their sensual histories. Cindy went back in time to search for a clue to her inability to access her sensual self. Ultimately she had a vivid memory of the birth of their child. She had begun to hemorrhage severely two or three days after the delivery, and the doctors urgently removed her uterus to save her life. Afterward, she had a long and difficult recovery with a newborn to take care of along with the psychological devastation of never being able to get pregnant again. Ever since then, Cindy had had a strong sense of being defective as a woman and had begun to shut down her sensual response to Stewart.

During this medical crisis, Stewart had felt impotent and so withdrew, further reinforcing the absence of sensual connection. This pattern was compounded when several years later Cindy had a large ovarian cyst, which again required emergency surgery. For the second time, Cindy felt defective physically as a woman and confronted as well the possibility of death during emergency surgery, this time in a foreign country.

In our session, Stewart held Cindy as she recalled the intense disappointment and sadness of her two operations. He told her of his fear of losing her and realized that he had become extracareful whenever he touched his wife, often refraining from becoming too passionate in his caress.

Meanwhile, once Cindy became more aware that she had been shutting off her sensuality for fear of feeling pain, she began to allow Stewart's slow, loving touch of her belly with its scars, her breasts, which hadn't been able to nurse, and her vagina and clitoris, which had both become numb. The flood-gates of sensuality opened for Cindy as she claimed an even deeper sense of her femininity than one based on her pelvic anatomy. Together they found the sensual dimension that had been lost in their sexual relationship, and they also had much more fun in bed!

Another example of sensual detachment was seen in Ray, who was unusual compared to most men that I see. He had never had a good feeling about his body. He had always wanted to make long, languid love with his wife, Caroline, but he knew that he had trouble being sensual and especially with receiving pleasure. Ray was heavy, and contrary to a lot of men who know they should lose some weight but do not let that interfere with their sexual sensuality, he believed that his body did not deserve sensual pleasure. Intrigued, I asked him about his childhood. Ray told me that as a boy his father had repeatedly beaten him. To escape the experience he learned to go into his fantasy mind and detach from his body. Often Ray would imagine himself being bigger so that he could prevent the beatings from his father and also protect his mother. So he began to eat, using food as a substitute for any real sensual connection to his body.

Caroline thankfully had a sensual and playful nature and wanted to pleasure Ray but couldn't get through the invisible shield that he had placed around his body. As the three of us explored the roots of this disconnection and Ray began to understand that this pattern of sensual detachment had begun in his childhood, he had what I call an Aha! experience. He saw how and why he'd become detached from his body. With this awareness he became more ready than he had ever been to allow Caroline to kiss, caress, massage, and make love to his body. At first it still felt uncomfortable, but keeping his eyes open and focused on Caroline's loving face helped him accept her affection, and slowly he began to let pleasure in, and he became increasingly free and joyful sexually.

Of course, pain that causes detachment and numbness may not be strictly physical abuse, as in the beatings in Ray's case, or a physical trauma, such as Cindy's. In fact, pain is actually more often emotional in origin. There are numerous cases of bad experiences shutting down sensual pleasure. In these cases the legacy of abuse makes a connection between body stimulation and fearful memories. How do we avoid remembering and reexperiencing these past traumas? One way is by detaching from the stimulus and simply not allowing ourselves to have the bodily sensations; in short, we go numb.

EMOTIONAL PAIN

Sarah and Phil were in love. It showed in the way they looked at each other in my office. They smiled often, touched hands, and had a soft, warm energy around them. To the naked eye, they seemed very much connected with their sensuality. They were planning on getting married in three months; it was a second marriage for both, and they felt certain that they had each found "the one." What they couldn't understand was why sex was not spectacular.

Sarah reported sadly that she couldn't really feel anything when Phil was making love to her. She knew that she loved him, but she had more intense feelings when they were just holding hands across a café table than when they were joining bodies. In previous relationships, Sarah had "faked it," but she was determined not to be an actress in this relationship. She wanted to be connected truthfully with Phil at all levels. Phil was at a loss, wanting nothing more than to share sensual pleasure with his fiancée. But no matter what he did, he couldn't break through the pervasive numbness that surrounded Sarah in bed.

I had certainly heard many similar stories before. I suspected that since Sarah deeply wanted to be sensual in this relationship but couldn't, she most probably had some type of emotional block. I began by asking Sarah about her past. What a past! She had grown up in a strict household with a defined set of expectations about the proper behavior of young women. This was not unusual or even particularly detrimental to her sense of self; rather, the real emotional pain came from her father, who had idolized her from the time she was "his baby." He not only showered her with attention and affection, which made Sarah's mother furious and jealous, he went over the line and had fondled Sarah's genitals for years. In addition, as she grew up, Sarah had to deal with her father's possessive rage whenever she dated. She even remembered when she was punished for unconsciously putting her hands between her legs one time when her boyfriend was at their house. Her father thought it was some type of erotic gesture.

By the time she met Phil ten years later, she'd become hypervigilant, willing to have sex, but unable to feel sexual. Like many women who have been abused, she had also developed the ability to leave her body during sex. She did not experience pain: she didn't experience anything!

However, because Sarah was so emotionally perceptive, she was able to see that Phil truly loved her. She could feel his warmth and love as they walked, talked, and laughed together. But during sex, the vigilant Sarah took over, and orgasm and sensual connection seemed impossible. Thankfully, Sarah was also courageous. By uncovering the source of the emotional pain *and* sharing the details with Phil, she experienced his steadfast commitment to her rather than the rejection she had feared when she revealed the truth of her sad childhood. She allowed him to begin healing her with his loving, sexual touch. By consciously getting back in connection with her body during sensual pleasuring, she blossomed into a beautifully sexual woman.

They sent me a wonderful picture taken on their wedding day, sitting in the Yab Yum position (more about that later) surrounded by clouds of her white wedding dress, beaming, clearly in touch and sensually connected.

Sexual abuse and sexual shame are incredibly common in our society. It makes my heart constrict every time I hear experiences such as Sarah's. For some women and men, these wounds never seem to heal, but the good news is that many individuals have successfully dealt with their emotional injuries and have reclaimed their sensuality and sexuality. If you are struggling with abuse or traumas, don't give up. There are many skilled practitioners who can help. And if you have now found a loving partner, my experience is that he or she is eager to help heal these scars and very much wants to be the one who brings back sensual enjoyment. In fact, the real shame in these situations is the ongoing injury to a healthy sex life. As I told Sarah, "Your father may have stolen your childhood, but he doesn't get to ruin your lifelong sexual joy if you banish him from your body memories." For her, reclaiming her sexuality became a crusade, a tenacious struggle against the old demons. She won. It is my hope that all women and men win this battle.

REVITALIZING YOUR SENSUAL DIMENSION

Exploring the sensual dimension requires becoming aware of the nuances of the different sensual aspects of our being as well as our partner's being. The sensual experience takes time; it is in the details of your touch of his face, or his caress of your breast, that sensual input expands sexuality. Hurrying the taste, the touch, the dance, shortchanges the power of sensory delights.

Of course, time is what none of us seems to have, so here are some specific suggestions or techniques that may help you to focus and explore the full range of your sensuality.

1. ADOPT A "SENSE OF THE WEEK"

Begin paying close attention to one particular sense for one week. The first sense that might be used would be touch. Put the word on the bathroom mirror or on the fridge. During this week, you might pay attention to the feeling of clothes against your skin, and, in fact, choose them because of how they feel on your body. You might notice the breeze on your face or pay close attention to the sensation you get when you shake someone's hand. Certainly, I would suggest that you schedule a massage during this week, if at all possible. The following week you might emphasize sound. Play music all week, listen to the rise and fall of a person's voice in conversation, and hear the wind in the trees. This delightful task will not only make you enjoy your day-to-day experiences more, but also definitely bring a more sensual self to bed. Take each sense in turn and either focus on it yourself, or, much more fun, do this exercise as a couple. Once you finish the six senses, you can begin again; sensual exploration is never-ending.

2. SENSES FOR FREE

Do something sensual that is free with your partner each day for two weeks. In other words, touch her, give her a sensual kiss, whisper in her ear when she least expects it. There is no need to respond sexually at that moment. This little sensual experience is "for free." Make a "goodie basket" of sensuality: have aromatherapy oils such as ylang-

ylang and lavender ready for use, put in a silken scarf to play with, add a long ostrich feather to tease the skin, put in a piece or two of exquisite chocolate, or even splurge on some chocolate body paint for you and your lover. The list of intriguing options is endless when we begin to include all of the senses.

3. UNEARTH PAST TRAUMA

Be honest with yourself and your partner about past trauma, especially if you have trouble relating to the sensual aspects of sexuality. If you have been abused, refuse to let it ruin the rest of your life as a sensual person. Were you ever hurt by someone during a sexual encounter? Did someone ever force you to have sex against your will? If so, understand first that you are not alone, then also that such traumas can have a profound effect on your sensual freedom. Resolve to reclaim that freedom. As in some of the examples above, merely using your present maturity to reexamine the incident may help. It can be important and helpful to share the trauma with your lover to allow him or her the opportunity to help heal the wound. However, professional assistance is also therapeutic, so do not delay in getting help if you are not making progress on your own.

4. GET OUT OF YOUR HEAD

If you are a person who lives "in your head," begin to discriminate about your sensibilities. Give yourself an assignment to notice what pleasures you. Linger over sensations, hang out with children who are definitely in their bodies, hang out with animals who are sensual creatures. In other words, develop sensuality as foreplay, your most exquisite skill for lovemaking.

5. CREATE A SANCTUARY OF BLISS

It's important for you and your lover to have a special place for sex. Whether you use your bedroom, a pleasant living area, or even the bathroom, you need a place where you can push aside worries and distractions to set the mood for sensuality and sexuality. By repeatedly using the same room for erotic encounters, you imbue that place with special associations. For instance, when you walk into the kitchen, you think of food. Elicit the senses and bring them into play with a piece of candy to share between mouths, erotic music, soft lighting, a subtle-scented candle, or a light incense. These sensual stimuli work on relaxing the body and mind, letting both you and your partner shed the worries and distractions of daily routines.

THE POWER OF THE SENSUAL

Awakening your body to the power of its sensual potential can be a wondrous, revitalizing journey. The body's sensuality can create a passion all its own, heightening the pleasure you give to each other and enriching your connection. Once the body is aroused in pleasure, its sensory channels open and charged with energy, both of you will feel like the most succulent strawberry in July, ripe and ready to be picked, savored, and enjoyed.

Think of your sensuality as a great gift that we have to understand and learn to take care of. It is the sensual that draws us to sex over and over. We make love for the pleasure of it, and therefore we need to become experts at the business of creating pleasure for our partner and—equally as important—learning how to receive sexual pleasure. The sensual canvas is vast and complex, and it is a true delight to explore the dimension with your lover.

Even as we get lost in languid sensuality, another energy is waiting in the wings, tapping its foot impatiently. What about desire, what about lust, what about sexual power? Desire is a force to be reckoned with, as we will see in the next dimension.

4

The Power of Lust

REFUELING YOUR DESIRE DIMENSION

THE URGE TO MERGE

The desire dimension is what we think of as hot sex. It is the wanting, the wanting to be wanted, the animallike energy that takes us over and makes us feel exhilarated by its power. It is what sells cars, cigars, makeup, and almost everything else in our society. It is the football captain and the prom queen, the alpha male and female. It is also about power: the power to influence our sexual partner and to surrender to the power of their sexual voodoo. We want that powerful passion, that tinge of the insatiable, that "I have to have him (or her)" quality simmering under the surface of our interactions.

When our relationship is brimming with lust, we feel more energy in every aspect of our life. When passion and desire are coursing through our sexual encounters with our lover, we feel as if the world could never end.

This aspect of our sexuality is rooted in and tied to animal mating behavior, and since we are mammals, we have these patterns as well. One incident that always reminds me of the power and the fundamental nature of the desire dimension took place one recent summer when I was taking a rafting trip down the Grand Canyon with my daughter. From the quiet, lazily drifting raft, my daughter and I looked up toward the sides of the canyon, where we observed a herd of mountain sheep. An older male ram, his head adorned with a huge double curl of horns, was strutting his stuff for the females. His behavior seemed to be saying, "Here I am, the best thing you'll ever see!"

All was well until a young ram, with only a single curl of horns, approached, obviously trying to attract the attention of one or two of the young ewes of the herd. Yet the older male was quite protective of his status, and soon the two males were fighting for dominance and the sexual right to the females.

What occurred to me as I watched this sexual encounter was how animal we humans continue to be. The basic need or urge to mate is what propels and energizes our attraction to our sexual partners. Human mating is more than coupling for reproduction; it is the drive to bond, to possess and be possessed. Therefore, when we connect in the desire dimension, we act upon deep, instinctual urges. Our code word for this urge is *lust*.

Your desire dimension picks up where the sensual leaves off. It is the engine that drives your sexual connection by taking the biologic potential of your body and fusing it with the sensuality that you've created with your six senses. As I mentioned earlier, the desire dimension is about power—the power to attract your lover and pull him or her into your irresistible web and the power to sweep both of you into animal lust. This lust is what fuels our passion, and it is what many of us assume will never last in a long-term relationship. Yet don't we want this passion to last forever?

The key to keeping lust and passion alive in your relationship is to free your inhibitions in order to tap into your sexual drive. Although one partner may have a stronger connection to his or her lust, if both of you work together to ignite desire, then that sexual electricity that may seem only a memory will return, and the magic can last throughout your relationship—no matter how long you've been together. If you have never been connected to your sexual lust, this chapter will help you identify the causes.

I have found that those couples whose desire dimension is powered by lust and passion share these essential qualities:

1. They delight in feeding their sexual connection throughout the day.
2. They know how to be sexually spontaneous and to let their passion flow.
3. They are confident of the power of their sexual attraction to each other.
4. They both initiate sex and know how to increase the sexual zest for each other.
5. They know how to enjoy juicy, noisy, exuberant, joyful sex.
6. They associate passion with positive, affirming images and beliefs.

WHAT HAPPENS TO THE SPARK?

Countless times, I have met couples who clearly describe their love for each other. They will be obviously committed to each other, and they cannot imagine being without the other. Yet, they will also describe their relationship as being without passion. They say that it is missing the spark, the fire. Like good roommates, they efficiently and amicably get the job of day-to-day living done, but miss out on the power of sex. Of course, there is nothing blatantly wrong with relationships such as these, but without a highly charged desire dimension, their sexual relationship is destined to feel bland, without excitement. Isn't this what we mean when we say sex has lost its spark?

In the early part of a relationship, we don't even doubt our desire for each other. We believe, in the throes of infatuation and new love, that our synergy, the fusion of the natural attractions we have for each other, is automatic and will last forever. This is what makes lust and desire so compelling and, at times, intoxicating. We cannot keep our eyes or our hands off one another. We feel those electrical sparks with even a casual touch and are hungry for our lover's body all the time. However, as the months go by, this lust tends to lose its edge, or sometimes to disappear altogether. For some of us, that the pursuit is over and that we actually possess our lover depletes the sexual energy.

When partners have been together for a long time, it is common for their sexual appetite to begin to wane. In our culture, we wryly comment that the "honeymoon is over" and accept that it is simply time to get down to the real business of living our lives together. The chase is over, the tension of whether he loves me, or she loves me, has been settled. That inning of the game has been played, and we then put aside our passion and look to our other, growing responsibilities. In other words, we begin to have desirous sex less and less.

You may live side by side with your partner; you eat together, go to family gatherings together, sleep together, but neither of you reaches across the bed to initiate sex. You begin to feel estranged and awkward. One partner may take on the role of initiator to no avail; the other partner cannot or will not respond. Now these two formerly sexually charged people have reached a sexual stalemate; both become resentful and detached. Remember, the one who wants sex the *least* is actually the one in control. Unless intercourse is actually being forced physically on the other (thankfully, this is not usually happening), it is the reluctant partner, the disinterested one, who has the excuses, the proverbial headache, and the control over whether sex happens or not.

Even if you have lost the spark, you may still be having sex in an effort to stay attached. But often your sex will have become mechanical, without enthusiasm or much pleasure. Couples may become virtually celibate, avoiding sex altogether. In fact, in recent years, I have seen more and more celibate relationships—couples who are having sex once every other month or perhaps four or five times a year. They have lost the magic, the urge to merge. For couples stuck in celibacy, it somehow seems better to read a good book than to try to get it on. The power of your attraction has leaked out of the sexual relationship, leaving you feeling empty.

In extreme situations, when this dimension gets very sidetracked, couples may use the sexual energy to manipulate their partner, using sex as a way to either punish or exert influence in another aspect of the relationship. "He's not going to get any you know what until . . ." "She has turned me down one too many times. I am going to wait her out and then see how she likes being ignored." The trust that is essential for healthy flirting, seduction, and lovemaking is not possible, and the disconnection between the partners has become filled with hostility, an indication that the desire dimension is in serious trouble, stuck in extreme negative energy.

How does this happen to us?

Sometimes the grind of everyday life steals our sexual juice. Even if we were once connected to this power center, we often lose it as the responsibilities of life pile on our shoulders. By merely going through the activities and chores of daily life, responding to one crisis after another, we lose track of our sexual lust and attraction. When we have detached from our sexual energy, we begin to move into celibacy. We no longer flirt with our honey; we no longer welcome his or her sexual attention. We don't give them a real kiss hello or good-bye. If our partner comes up behind us when we are at the kitchen sink and begins to nuzzle our neck, instead of arching back into his or her body, which would invite further touch and progression of the connection, we close down and push our partner away. We complain of there being "no time" for lovemaking, or in some cases, we are so sexually shut down that we are afraid to encourage our man or woman because we are trapped in the despair of the celibate space. We are afraid that having sex will be so disappointing it will only further the distance between us.

But you don't have to give in to the default of celibacy. Every one of us can learn how to keep the spark alive and to fuel the passion forever.

DID YOU EVER HAVE THE SPARK?

THE CONFIDENCE FACTOR IN THE MATING GAME

Women and men expend a great deal of energy attracting a mate. It can be fun, naughty, and certainly exhilarating. Yet to join the mating game, we need confidence in ourselves and in our attractiveness. One of the components that positively energizes the desire dimension is sexual confidence. When our sense of confidence to "play the game" is weakened or shattered, a relationship can quickly become depleted of its lust.

Did you feel inadequate to the task of sexual attraction in your adolescent or young-adult years? Were you unable to "get" the guy or girl you longed to be with? Those experiences can be searing to our souls, and as adults, we may never feel adequate entering this arena again. Perhaps you were ridiculed because of your body or some other aspect of your sexuality. For instance, Karen, a thirty-year-old manager of a hotel, came to see me for help becoming less inhibited with her husband. She said her husband found her closed down sexually. She explained that internally she wanted to be more open and less inhibited and had even gone out and bought some sex toys, such as edible powder, feathers, and other items to introduce into their sexual play. But even though she and her husband laughed at her efforts, which broke some of the tension around the issue, she still felt "bottled up inside."

Together, we went through the dimensions to evaluate how she and her husband related to one another. When we got to the desire dimension, she realized that she was not a confident, powerful lover. When I asked her why, especially since she knew her husband was attracted to her body and thought her sexy, Karen began searching through her early feelings about her attractiveness as a female. She remembered quite vividly an episode on the playground when she was in the seventh or eighth grade. There was a wild, fun game of tag ball going on with a group of boys and girls. When she triumphantly found the lost ball under a bush (being small enough to scramble underneath) and waved it in the air, an older boy said sarcastically, "Do you want a medal, or a chest to pin it on!" These wounding words went straight to the heart of Karen's emerging femininity.

In retrospect, she knew that this was a harmless remark about her as yet undeveloped body—not meant to really hurt her. But over twenty years later, she remembered the insult as clearly as if it were yesterday.

Many of us may recall similar slights. (I remember being referred to as a "board" by a boy in junior high and thought my breasts inferior for years before I threw out my padded bras with my hip-huggers and Flower Power pins!) For Karen, the experience became internalized as a belief that she was sexually inadequate. The task for many of us is to recognize and understand our internal sexual profiles and then to reassess and adjust them. If these images of ourselves are negative, they may be responsible for inhibiting our ability to feel sexual desire and to initiate sex.

On the other hand, when we feel good and accepting of ourselves, including our bodies, we feel confident, and this confidence is directly tied to feeling free to be sexual. A persistently negative body image, no matter how it came about, is one of the factors that make men and women feel inadequate. We live in a culture that seems fixated on physical fitness and beauty; we are given a prescription for a singularly unrealistic image of a female who is young, thin, tall, and buxom, and a male who is strong, muscled, flat-stomached, and otherwise invincible. Therefore, it is not difficult to feel that we fall short of this "ideal beauty." If we use this media-generated ideal as some form of comparison (whether consciously or unconsciously) for ourselves, we are setting ourselves up for disaster. If we don't like the way we look or if we think that our partner isn't turned on by how we look, that negative feeling will inhibit our lust and desire. We will shut down, turn off, and avoid sex altogether.

Mark and Trish, a couple in their midforties, highlight the destructive power of these internal images. Otherwise a loving, committed couple, they had found themselves in a stalemate of inaction, not able to risk initiating sex and becoming more and more anxious about their increasingly infrequent sex. Both of them stated that they would like to be making love more often, approximately three or four times a week, but that their busy lives selling real estate made this impossible. In actuality, they were making love only about once a month.

In our session, Mark admitted that he never initiated sex anymore because of repeated rejections years ago from Trish. This had all started one time when he had asked Trish at the beginning of lovemaking, "Have you been gaining some more weight, honey?" Angry, hurt, and extremely self-conscious, Trish had begun to refuse Mark's advances. Once Trish withdrew, Mark gradually got to the point where he could no longer bear the humiliation of "begging for it," as he put it. He decided he'd rather wait for Trish to initiate sex. She interrupted him at this point and asked him, how was she supposed to initiate sex when she felt that she was no longer sexually appealing to him? She reminded him that his questions about her weight were hurtful.

Trish admitted that she had always been concerned about her body shape, and she pointed to areas of cellulite on her thighs and belly, long-standing sources of her feeling inadequate. Mark, however, adamantly stated that he still found himself turned on by his wife daily, but he didn't know how to convince her of her sexual appeal. He tried again to assure her that his comments about her weight didn't affect his sexual attraction to her. In fact, he was quick to point out that he too had put on weight with age.

The two of them were in touch with their emotional love for each other, and they obviously had a wonderful foundation. But it was also apparent that they had let their sexual connection dwindle. Mark's seeming lack of interest had reinforced Trish's poor body image. And he had become stubborn about not initiating, choosing to stay stuck in the "poor me" role. Naturally, Trish's hyper-self-consciousness made her completely averse to initiating.

In counseling and treating them, I encouraged them to cut a sexual deal by crafting a contract in which each of them would take turns initiating sex. It wasn't a question of how many times, but a question of who would do the initiating each week for a month (see "Cut a Deal" in the "Tools" section below). I also suggested some other exercises geared toward getting Trish in touch with—and improving—her sexual self-image, so she could build her confidence in the attractiveness of her voluptuous body.

Within a month, I had received a call from them, saying that they had not only renewed an active sex life, but that Trish had begun to allow Mark to love and touch her, which in turn encouraged Mark to begin initiating sex more spontaneously. Their stalemate had resulted from neither of them wanting to risk rejection. They had been hiding from each other because of this fear of rejection and had been unable to let go and return to the delight and passion of their earlier connection.

For this dimension of their sexual relationship to heal and become reenergized, it was necessary first that Trish believe that she was attractive to Mark, and second that Mark reinforce that belief by initiating sex in a playful, meaningful way. Sexual confidence is what can lead you back into the mating game.

SHEDDING THE SKIN OF INHIBITION

Feeling uninhibited and free to express desire and lust is one of the foundations of a positively charged desire dimension. We all seem to know someone—a man or a woman—who seems so safe, free, and at ease in his or her own skin. We may not know these people intimately, but we imagine that they are great, passionate lovers. Why are some of us more uninhibited and spirited than others?

If you feel that you may want to shed the restricting skin of inhibition, then you will need to examine your inner beliefs or associations about sex. I can think of many women who have come to me to discuss problems they have had in handling their husband's desire, but one woman in particular comes to mind. After six years of marriage, Bonnie said she was unable to be responsive in sex, despite feeling attracted to her husband. Most of the time, her husband ended up masturbating because she could not make herself have sex with him "just for his sake." When I asked her why she didn't want to have sex, she explained haltingly that once he was naked and erect, she found herself repulsed by her husband's desire. Where had her own sexual desire been buried?

When I questioned Bonnie further, asking her about her background and her sexual experiences before marriage, I found out two interesting facts. First, Bonnie was raised as one of four daughters in a fairly strict household. From the time she was little, she had learned that sex, this strange thing that men and women did together, was something that you had to do to become a mother, but that the sex act itself was disgusting. She had also learned that a woman had to put up with a man's need to have sex in order for them to stay together. Within their house, Bonnie said, her mother often berated her father if he walked around in his boxers or even came out of his bathroom with a towel wrapped around him. The presence of her father's partially naked body was considered alarming in their house, and there seemed to be the underlying belief that all men were dominated by unfortunate biological needs and that they were therefore untrustworthy.

After further discussion, Bonnie linked these early memories of her mother's constant criticism and discomfort with her husband's body to her own discomfort with her husband. He was one of those untrustworthy, faintly disgusting men with one of those scary penises! Bonnie and I laughed as we discussed the drama that had surrounded this issue in her childhood home. I assured her that she could choose a different attitude toward nakedness and male physicality from that of her mother. But I also encouraged her to work with the tools and practice replacing these negative images of sex with positive ones. She also consciously focused on her first sense-filled encounters with the man she had married. This too helped put her in touch with her bodily pleasure. Gradually, she was able to discard the early beliefs she had automatically adopted and discover her attraction to her husband. Ultimately, she was able to welcome her husband's desire for her *and* feel her own innate desire for him and his body, even with his "scary" penis.

Is your sexual self in the closet? Bringing that self out from where she has so often been banished early in our lives is one of the most exciting steps a woman can take. As you unlock the door and begin to enjoy your hidden sexual self, you will experience a fabulous rush of vitality and feel alive. Now you will be in a place where you can meet and match your partner's enthusiasm, thereby fueling his passion and ardor without shame and self-judgment.

THE POWER OF THE EROTIC

Paris has lovers kissing in the street, and India has wonderful sensual drawings of sacred lovemaking in a multitude of positions. Many movies have a memorable scene or two with hot love. These all represent the erotic, the sensual pathway from our mind to our body. The erotic has the power to trigger our senses and get us sexually aroused—if we are open to it. Reading a breathless, sexual story to our lover can quickly take us to the sensual world via detailed description. Certainly the romance novels make heavy use of the erotic to energize their stories and to keep us awake late at night, looking for one more thrill.

I believe in the power of erotica as a key to the desire dimension. There are now even some tasteful films and videos (which in a store or catalog may be classified as pornography) that can really get the juices flowing! I encourage couples to use whatever tools they like to open and fuel their desire dimension.

However, a problem can occur when such devices are used too often and end up disrupting your connection to your sensuality or blocking your ability to connect with your partner's sensuality. For instance, I had one patient who came to me because she no longer felt "sexy" with her husband. She had closed down sexually after he had become too reliant on pornographic magazines. It made her feel left out because he seemed disconnected from her. Earlier in their relationship, he'd introduced the magazines as a way to have fun and spice up their sex life, and she had gone along with reading *Penthouse* and *Playboy* as a way to explore sexual arousal.

But as time went on, her husband seemed to become more and more reliant on this outside stimulation to get an erection and have an orgasm. Every time they had sex, he would look at a magazine. My patient not only felt replaced by the impossibly endowed women in the magazines, but also that her husband was not really present when they made love. She was sure he was off on an extended sexual fantasy that did not include her.

In this case, I suggested that they both come in for a couples counseling session. I first asked my patient's husband if he still felt sexually connected to his wife and whether he felt he was too dependent on the porn magazines for sexual stimulation. He responded that he was very attracted to her and that he only used the magazines because he thought they both enjoyed them. He hadn't realized that they were having such a negative effect on her.

In this case, the pornography had become a sign of their disconnection in the lust dimension: he went into fantasy and she into accommodation mode. Since they both agreed they were very sensual beings, highly aware of touches, smells, sights, and sounds, I suggested they embark on the "sense of the week" and "senses for free" techniques (from the previous chapter). I encouraged them to opt for more literary erotica and perhaps stay away from the "pictures." Reading erotica or sexy stories can be fun and arousing, and generally not as sexually distancing as pictures to some women. Bringing the sensual aspects of erotica to each other was now part of the plan.

As with anything, repeatedly watching porno films or reading stories about other people getting it on can become boring or almost a sexual bypass to a real desire-filled experience where lovers are present for each other. Erotica in all its forms is a powerful way to get in touch with your desire, but be sure to discover how to share this fluid feeling with your lover.

THE PRIMITIVE POWER OF LUST

Lust, deeply primitive and spontaneous, makes many of us feel out of control. Some of us may have experienced our partner's out-of-control lust, which can have for us the sexy quality of "being taken" but can sometimes turn into forced sex, which is scary. We like to think that we have come further along the evolutionary path than the rams and ewes, but feeling such intense desire can be unnerving. The conflict between letting go (releasing) this energy and the fear of losing control is what also makes lust a two-edged sword. At the same time, the tension between these two forces is what fuels that electric feeling we remember from our thrilling sexual encounters.

If women are taught that the sexual drive or lust is despicable and frightening (such as Bonnie above), they will see the desire (or lust) of their man as perverted, animalistic, and uncontrolled. They identify this lust with a male in an aggressive posture. What happens next? Women feel repelled by what they've been conditioned to avoid and thus shut down. This prevents them from connecting with their own sexual power or drive. As women mature sexually, they can often begin to accept that they do have their own sexual drive, and that they can be sexually powerful too without dominating or manipulating their partner. They can also accept and welcome their male partner's more visceral brand of sexual desire and feel invigorated by it—instead of afraid or repelled.

Because men and women are often raised differently (with almost opposing attitudes toward their sexuality), they often find themselves at odds in this dimension of the relationship—with the woman acting as the gatekeeper to sex while positioning the man as the desirer, barely able to control his sexual urges. At the same time, since men are traditionally the ambassadors of this dimension, in charge of all initiation of sex, women tend to wait and follow their lead.

This pattern may work fine within a relationship, but the danger is that women can begin to manipulate their man by withholding sex (remember, the one who wants sex the *least* is the one in control), and the man can become resentful of his woman. Sexually, he may become even more one-dimensional because he's seeking to satisfy his "animal" urges while his partner just wants him to hurry up and get it over with. How dismal! Men in this situation often try to beat the odds: they may assume a 10 percent return on their efforts, so they reason that if they initiate one hundred times, they will get it ten times! And, as everyone knows, something is better than nothing.

Let me tell you a story of what can happen when we act out this fear of uncontrolled sexual urges and disconnect love and desire. In this case, the woman wasn't afraid of her man's uncontrolled lustful urges, but of her own. Marty came to see me greatly upset about having just ruined her relationship with her fiancé. A few weeks before she was to marry the man she loved, she had had a one-night stand with a man who was handsome but a virtual stranger! Marty described their sexual encounter as "hot" and charged with excitement. Once we began to talk about her regret for her actions, I asked if she had this same kind of exhilarating sex with her fiancé. She shyly said, "No." When I asked her if she knew why not, she explained that though she wanted to, she just couldn't let herself go with him. She didn't want him to see that "side" of her.

As we talked further, Marty described how she was afraid that if she let go sexually, her fiancé wouldn't continue to love her. I pointed out that she seemed to be demonstrating a belief in an inherent conflict between feelings of love and those of sexual desire. Her one-night stand was a way of acting out this split between love and sex: she was able to let go sexually with the man she didn't love, but not with the man she did love.

She was so confused and appalled with herself that she called off the wedding. She realized that she couldn't go through with the marriage if she was not able to give all of herself to her fiancé.

Marty's belief that uninhibited sexual passion and love are incompatible stems from a larger, more pervasive belief that sexual desire is bad or wrong. Until she is able to unearth and shed her negative associations toward sexual desire, she will continue to repeat the splitting behavior. One part of her was good, and one part of her was baaad. Are you like Marty? Do you see love and sexual desire as being at odds with each other rather than just different components of the whole relationship? If so, you may find it difficult to be passionate with your soul mate. But, while Marty described the loss of her relationship as tragic, ultimately she was grateful that she understood her internal dynamic. She is now looking for a man with whom she can be in love and in lust!

ARE YOU A MIDLIFE VIRGIN?

Sometime these negative beliefs about sex are so deeply implanted in women's psyches, they may not rear their heads until later on in life, after a woman has successfully navigated the dating and mating game. I call this woman the midlife virgin.

She is a woman who has had intercourse many times. She has probably had children, and yet she is still virginal in her approach to her sexuality. Instead of harnessing and unleashing her sexual desire, she keeps it quietly (yet actively) tucked away for fear of its overtaking her. She has not claimed her own power. She has not taken this energy for herself or given it back to her partner. She is still too highly invested in the image of herself as a "good girl." In fact, if she identifies with her lustful desire, she sees herself as either being ungovernable or opening the door to being taken advantage of sexually, which will only lead her to sinful behavior or inevitable harm. Again, this is related to lust's association with losing control, as if this kind of desire will be bigger and stronger than your power to make the decision to use it when you want.

Sometimes the midlife virgin emerges with motherhood. Edith, a young new mother, described retreating from her husband, John, sexually after the birth of her twin boys. Before their birth, and in the early years of their courtship and marriage, they had had a healthy sexual relationship, marked by both of them initiating sex often, at least two or three times a week. Now, after five years of marriage, no matter what her husband did or said to encourage her sexuality, it wasn't enough to overcome the guilt that she had regarding her sexual desire. As a result, Edith began actively avoiding sex: she went to bed before her husband, she complained of feeling exhausted, that she wasn't "clean"—any excuse she could come up with. By the time she reached out for counseling, she was so upset by the conflict over sex in her marriage that she could barely speak through her tears for the first ten minutes.

When she finally calmed down and began to talk, she told me something else I thought was interesting. Edith said that over the past few years, she had also become irrationally jealous of other women's attention to her husband, making John more frustrated and helpless. She was aware that she was not satisfying his sexual needs, and she was petrified that some other woman would. She was trapped in a morass of self-blame and despair.

As Edith and I discussed her frustration over being afraid to let go, she realized that she believed that having sex somehow sullied her ability to be a good mother. This belief implied that sex is some kind of purveyor of badness or sinfulness. Although Edith wasn't sure where she had learned this association, she suspected it was from her mother, whom Edith described as having had sex only twice in her life—once to have Edith and once for her sister. Edith cared deeply about her moral responsibility as a mother. She was petrified that her boys would catch her and her husband having sex (she didn't call it "making love"), and she even changed her way of dressing to become matronly much before her time. She had become a midlife virgin even though she had originally been much more free sexually. Edith is not alone in encountering hidden beliefs that arise unexpectedly with different life stages.

To her credit, Edith could see that she did not wish to remain a midlife virgin. Through our work together, she became able to connect her deep love for her husband with her desire to pleasure him and herself. During the homework assignment she reconnected with her lust and even let John pleasure her sexually while he spoke to her about how much he loved her. She surprised herself by having several orgasms during this session of lovemaking. John was not only immensely pleased by her renewed responsiveness to his touch, but also felt he had recovered the woman he had not seen in many years. They both began to see desire as the engine that could fuel the physical expression of their durable love.

THE RELUCTANT MAN

While males are more commonly seen as the aggressors in our sexual relationships, men can be passive, or reluctant to assume their sexual power. Is this due to waning testosterone in the male, as we saw in the biologic dimension? Or to embarrassment about erectile dysfunction? These are only two of the reasons. Are you one of the many women who initiate most or all of their sexual encounters? This commonly occurs in couples of all ages and is even more frequent in midlife couples. Ironically, many women may be coming into their own sexual power in midlife—just as their man may be tiring of the role of initiator.

Such a shift in the power dynamics between partners is not necessarily problematic unless the woman begins to feel uncomfortable in her desire and unloved or unappreciated by her reluctant partner, or unless the man feels frustrated with his difficulty in initiating sex. For many couples, this dynamic works for them; they are comfortable and satisfied by their respective roles. However, if one of you is frustrated with this sharp division between initiator and receiver, then you may want to examine some of the underlying reasons for these choices.

Have you ever found yourself hinting that tonight would be a great night for making love, and he is distracted, catching up on E-mails? You have put on that sexy little number and he pretends not to notice. In my work as a sexual counselor this situation is surprisingly common. Yet women who feel more sexually desirous than their mate have little social support in our society, which is committed to the image of the guy chasing the reluctant woman around the bedroom. As a result, a woman in the role of initiator may begin to feel sexually scorned, feeling rejected because her lover does not respond to her advances or always makes her initiate sex.

What is this woman's choice? Suppress her sexual drive, become angry and bitter, find a lover? None of these choices are good. We need to see what may be at the root of a man who gets detached from his sexual self.

Tom, a fifty-year-old physician, came to see me because his wife was frustrated that he seemed to leave all their sexual encounters up to her. When I questioned him why he didn't like to initiate, we uncovered how he had developed his sexual profile. He recalled a memory of himself as a frustrated young man, standing against the wall in his room, with his hands held tightly behind him. He then linked this image to his fear of being violent or too physical with his hands. Tom vividly remembered the tempestuous relationship between his tyrannical stepfather and his docile, "sweet" mother. He said his mother was near to "sainthood," and he hated the man in her life. His stepfather used physical force and domination daily.

Tom desperately wanted to avoid identifying with his stepfather, because he was determined never to be like this man. He knew that his mother felt forced to sexually accommodate her husband, and this bothered Tom tremendously. Some part of him vowed never to require that of a woman he married. As a young man, Tom had systematically renounced his physical power and never learned how to engage or appreciate his sexual desire. Thus, his sexual passivity was an expression of his deeply held belief that sex and love do not go together, that goodness and sensual desire are antagonists.

Men can also respond to internalized negative teachings that shut down their lust. Matt and his wife of twenty years came in to discuss the gradual diminishment of sex in their relationship over the years. Matt, from the beginning, had admired Kristy's sexuality, although he admitted being overwhelmed by her sexual drive at the onset of their marriage. He had been raised in a stern Catholic family and was trained and educated by strict Jesuits. He vividly remembered the shame of his mother catching him masturbating in his bedroom. For Matt, sex was always something to be done in secret, a furtive act that occurred when you couldn't control your "base," almost subhuman needs.

Matt was aware of and attracted to Kristy's open, lustful passion, which she had learned from her well-adjusted parents' loving and committed marriage. However, for Matt, sex and shame remained inseparable. He found it difficult to get an erection unless he was self-stimulating. To consider sex the ultimate manifestation of the love he had for Kristy went against all of his training.

Gradually, Matt became less ashamed of his sexuality and more open to the fun and energy of the desire dimension. I also suggested he refer to some of the books that I recommend in the resource section to give him some ideas of how to pleasure his wife while he kept consciously working to connect his love for her with his desire. Over several sessions, Kristy was delighted with the playfulness that began to emerge from Matt. Here finally was the sexual partner she had always wished for.

The causes of sexual passivity or celibacy are specific to each individual—male or female. What we see in Tom's and Matt's cases is the way negative beliefs or sexual experiences direct future sexual interactions. What's important for reenergizing the lust or desire of your sexual relationship is to become aware of who you think you are sexually. You can enhance your sexual-desire profile by looking for ways to be lighthearted with lust. Teasing your lover, flashing him or her while beaming a wicked grin, surprising him or her with a new location or position, amps up the connection and helps to feed this dimension. So, whoever carries the energy in this dimension needs the applause of their partner. We need to "love the lusty one!" (See the tools section.)

EXTERNAL HUMILIATIONS KILL SEXUAL URGES

I can't count the times I've heard how a failure at work or in a career has negatively affected a sexual relationship! This pattern is especially common with men. Let me give you this example: Sherry and Gerald, a couple in their midforties from the Northwest, came to see me after Gerald had for months been unable to maintain an erection. This had led him to stop initiating sex, and finally to withdrawing from sex altogether. They were entering their sixth month of celibacy. I learned that Gerald had declared bankruptcy the year before, and their bank had repossessed all of Gerald and Sherry's assets. They had lost everything—the house, the car, most of their valuable belongings—and they had had to start over again. Even though this horrible experience had taken place quite a while before our conversation, Gerald was still emotional as he described his foreclosure hearing.

Both Sherry and Gerald knew that his not being able to perform sexually was related to his damaged self-esteem and his career stress. During our sessions, Sherry quietly observed that she had learned something important about herself through this crisis. She had found a strength and a belief in herself that had carried her through. She knew now that she had the power to create her own happiness, no matter what her external or financial circumstances might be. However, Gerald had not been so lucky in his insight. He found it difficult to accept that Sherry loved him for his inner being, and not for what he could provide her. He couldn't believe that without his double ram's curl she would still want to be his mate. He had lost his sense of personal power and had retreated so completely from her that he hadn't even wanted to come in to discuss the sex issue.

Sherry had only succeeded in dragging him in because she refused to accept that their once dynamic sexual relationship was over. We discussed in depth the sense of failure Gerald felt, even though financially he was now back on his feet. He needed to hear again how much Sherry loved him for who he was and not what he could give her. Finally he accepted that using Viagra for his erections might help him over the "hump" and jump-start a fuller, more meaningful recovery as he and Sherry became sexually active again.

Even in their celebration of the return of their sexual connection, neither of them could quite believe the directness of the connection between Gerald's sexual ability, the loss of his desire, and the humiliation of his financial setback. If you notice that your lover or partner has started to avoid sex after a recent business setback or failure, then gently point out the connection between the two events. Sometimes the simple awareness of the connection is enough to remedy the problem. However, if the problem persists or feels overwhelming to either or both of you, then I would try sifting through all your dimensions, paying particular attention to underlying beliefs about sexuality. These are often the deep-rooted causes of sexual problems.

Men, more so than women, are raised under pressure to "perform," and their manhood and masculinity is often tied to their physical and sexual prowess. Viewing (either consciously or unconsciously) sex as a performance sport, however, leads many men to confuse any kind of performance with that in the bedroom. If they have a bad day at work, if they lose a job, don't receive a promotion, or go bankrupt, they will funnel this sense of inadequacy or failure into their sexual relationship. The direct result is typically to withdraw or stop initiating sex entirely. "Who wants to start something that you can't finish?" they tell me when their erections are fickle.

But both women and men are equally vulnerable to the power of external humiliation. One striking example I encountered is of a young woman who, many years earlier at the age of nineteen, had gotten pregnant by her equally young boyfriend. Her parents made her get an abortion, and although they paid for it, they put enormous pressure on her to pay them back the money, which at that time was a substantial sum to her. It took the young woman years to pay back her parents, and during that time her parents hounded her for the money and used this as an excuse to punish her over and over for her mistake.

When I met her ten years later to discuss her lack of desire and her inability to be sexually free with her passionate husband, she told me that the trauma was not the abortion itself but her parents' unrelenting pressure about the money, which had so reinforced her shame that she had become completely unable to open herself to sexual abandonment—the very thing that had caused the unplanned pregnancy so many years earlier.

External humiliations have potent power to affect our sexuality. It is up to you to be aware of how these experiences affect you, so that they do not stifle the passion in your relationship.

ENERGIZE YOUR DESIRE

Wherever couples find themselves on the continuum of the desire dimension, it's important to become aware of how you are relating to each other in terms of your desire or lust. Many problems are situational and can therefore be addressed simply by becoming aware of how external life factors get channeled into your sex life. Other problems stem from more interior, personal issues.

As we've seen throughout this chapter, when many of us experience problems in the desire dimension, we are stuck in its static, middle space. What we often don't realize is how much energy we expend just staying stuck. We will feel drained and exhausted, overwhelmed by the mere thought of trying to reconnect with our own desire or respond to our partner's. I have come up with specific suggestions for transforming this area and energizing it in a more positive direction.

TOOLS FOR EXPANDING THE DESIRE DYNAMIC

1. LOVE THE LUSTY ONE

In a couple, one partner tends to be the "keeper of the flame." This is natural, so try to recognize, accept, admire, and appreciate the partner who has the stronger sexual drive. If you are guilty of berating or belittling your partner for his or her sexual lust, consider instead the radical act of thanking them for bringing that dimension to your relationship. Chances are that if your partner's desire is appreciated, he or she will be able to relax and not feel so compelled or under so much pressure to initiate sex. As a result, your sexual encounters will feel more equal and spontaneous.

Begin to consider your responsibility in activating the desire dimension and try one sensual act with your partner every day for the next two weeks, whether it is an erotic caress or simply saying that you appreciate his or her sexuality.

2. RECLAIM THE EROTIC

Notice your immediate response to sensations that remind you of sex. For example, eat a slippery, soft mango, or become aware of the musky, earthy smell of your genitals. Place a length of a banana in your mouth; what do you experience? Is the feeling one of enjoyment or of anxiety, or of amusement? Begin to energize this dimension by reclaiming the erotic. Be on the lookout for erotic, sensual movies. Become aware of loving couples and notice how they touch, speak, and look at each other. Use your everyday experiences to arouse your erotic energy and to keep you in touch with what turns you on. To heighten your awareness, write down something each day for the next month that you noticed was erotic, whether it's a piece of clothing at the mall, a picture in a magazine, or the luscious touch of some fabric. Think of these experiences as part of a personal makeover that will be shared with your lover in a myriad of ways in the future.

3. BANISH SHAME

Acknowledge humiliation when it occurs—whether it is outside the relationship or within it. Then begin to take steps to use sexuality to heal an episode of humiliation or shame, such as business setbacks, troubles with children or in-laws, or social embarrassments. Sex can be very healing for the disappointments of life. Remember that those endorphins released with orgasm have great power to change our outlook on the troubles of the day. It is also important to be reminded that as bad as things might be, you still have each other and sex can be used as a way to reaffirm your connection. One woman I know developed a fantastic (although unorthodox) treatment for her husband's major business crisis. When he came home each evening during this period, she would take him into the bedroom, undress him, and instruct him to lie down on the bed, then would hold his balls softly and protectively—because all day long everybody else had been trying to cut them off! I can't help smiling when I think of this, but what a terrific, symbolic gesture that demands little from him.

4. BE SEXUALLY HONEST

Avoid shaming or humiliating your partner when he or she does express desire or lust. Try to welcome your partner's energy and accept it. Begin to investigate where your ideas about sexual desire originated. Are you the midlife virgin? The sexually passive male? Why? Where did you learn that attitude? When did it begin? Though we often change many of the attitudes we hold about economics, politics, and child-rearing as we go through life, our early, formative beliefs about sex can be incredibly tenacious.

5. EXPRESS YOUR LUST

If you trust your partner (and this is essential), begin to explore your sexual power. "Take" your partner, make lots of noise during lovemaking, or become openly seductive. Even more important, let your partner try such a seduction of you. Even if you feel resistant, play along and see where the experience takes you. Rock-hard resistance to change leads you absolutely nowhere.

6. CUT A DEAL FOR SEXUAL WEALTH

One approach that can break a cycle of celibacy is what I call "cutting a deal." Think of your sexual relationship as you do your future savings: you need a long-term plan requiring attention, nurturing, and the desire for continued growth. When we take sex as seriously as we do many of the other aspects of our life, such as our career and our financial future, we can take a much more focused and goal-oriented approach to our sexual connection. Start by creating a "good sex division" of your relationship: envision what the two of you want sexually and then put it down on paper in as much detail as possible. Then carve out time to create a plan that puts this vision into place. By putting this in writing it becomes a contract that binds you to it. For example, you may agree that each one of you initiates sex for the next month (a week is too short and longer than a month undermines the plan). The initiator gets to call the shots and may choose the sensual or sexual setting accordingly: use candles, flowers, and music if you are romantic. If you are more sensual, you might use a new massage oil or get out the vibrator to stimulate each other. If you are even more adventuresome, you may decide to initiate sex in another room in the house or on the back porch. In any case, the individual who initiates sex is responsible for making sure that the sexual encounter happens.

A common problem is that we believe throughout the day that we really want to make love this very night, and then when the evening comes, we find ourselves too tired or we get into a spat, which makes us disinclined to make love. To honor the contract, you need to be able to begin a sexual encounter from a zero level of desire.

I often use the analogy of exercise. Don't you push yourself to exercise even when you don't feel like it? Don't you do it knowing that, after your work out, you'll feel better—both in your body and your mind? It is the same with sex. We don't always feel "in the mood," but usually after we're one or two steps into it, we're glad to be there and often relieved.

Try this for one month, then the two of you need to schedule a "board meeting" to discuss how the new sex division is working. At the board meeting, the agenda is to review the past month, discussing which experiences were pleasurable, which taught you something new about yourself or one another, and which didn't work. Then you can decide to extend the contract, change the terms, add a bonus clause, or in some way modify your original agreement. It is important not to discuss each sexual occurrence at the time, but instead wait until the end of the month. You need a month to gather the data.

DESIRE'S DOMAIN

When we claim to be bored by relationships, we are often talking about the absence or waning of the seductive energy. While real life and its complexities and responsibilities can and will distract us from being continuously seductive or receptive to our partner, we need to continue to look at our history and internalized beliefs about sex. Even in long-term relationships, I don't think we can underestimate the continued power of the way we were initiated into the mating game. If in looking at your sexual self you find shame and awkwardness, it makes sense that you want to withdraw, feeling rejected or too vulnerable to try to get in touch with your lust. Yet no matter what the problem is, with awareness and work it's more than possible to reverse any dynamic and embrace desire in an active, passionate way.

Lust is powerful energy and needs to be kept alive and active in a relationship for the partners to thrive. By reenergizing their lust connection, partners will feel not only invigorated, but closer. The shared sense of intimacy and freedom that comes from unleashing physical desire has a unique way of pushing a couple into all realms of possible pleasure and sexual enjoyment. When couples actively commit to keeping their desire alive, the passionate thrill of those early sexual encounters can last a lifetime.

5

Merging Sex and Love in the Four-Chambered Heart

EXCEPTIONAL SEX

Jill could not understand herself. "I don't get it," she said. "Seven years ago I was in this incredibly passionate relationship. We could not keep our hands off each other. I was a wild woman!

"Of course, I knew from the start that I didn't love him. He was gorgeous and he absolutely drooled over me, but I always realized that this was a short-term thing. Now I am married to a man I truly love. Bobby is handsome and attentive. We have a beautiful daughter, and I know that he is the one for me." Then Jill got a frown on her face. "But I just cannot seem to let go sexually with him. It is almost as if I love him too much!"

Jill could not understand, at first, why she could have so much lust for one man whom she didn't love and so much love for a man whom she couldn't let see her lust. I challenged her,

"What would happen if you let Bobby see your wild, sexual self?"

Jill looked at me. "I don't know. I can't think why that would be a problem."

"Don't try to think it through. Imagine being openly sexual, the way you were with your old lover."

After a moment, Jill's eyes widened. "Oh," she said softly. "I get it. If I am out there sexually with Bobby and I love him as much as I do, he gets all of me! I am not holding anything back. I am totally vulnerable and I have nothing left to bargain with."

Sound familiar? How can we blend sex and love, lust and love, getting it on and getting in touch? "He wears his heart on his sleeve." "She is all heart." "He is heartless." "She broke my heart." Countless phrases such as these weave through our language as testimony to the importance of love as a vital and vulnerable connection between humans. When our heart connection is strong, our sexual bond becomes more firmly rooted in our commitment to each other and therefore has greater meaning and depth.

One of the reasons the phrases about the heart are so prevalent in our language is because we do actually experience the emotion of love in the physical space occupied by our heart. When we feel these sensations, then we begin to give meaning to that often ambiguous and misused phrase "being in love."

When the passion of sex meets the energy of love, we create a bonfire of emotion. You glide through your daily routine beaming with inner joy, feeling expansive, openhearted, and continuously connected to your lover. What an intoxicated, intense experience being in our heart is! How enticing is this blissful connection! And how much we desire to capture this feeling forever!

Have you ever noticed couples who seem to have mastered the skill of being openhearted? These are couples who seem to embody the spirit of generosity and are genuinely pleased with the successes of their partner, able to admire their partner without feeling personally threatened. "She's the best thing that has ever happened to me." "Isn't he something? I am so proud of him." "We are so lucky to have found each other." They are the ones who are gazing fondly at each other at other people's weddings as if they are the ones getting married. These couples seem to take immense pleasure in simply being with each other; they feel complete and satisfied in their relationship. Notice the aura around these couples. It is usually comfortable, warm, soft, and is often filled with humor.

I refer to these couples as having an "easy love." They tend to laugh, tease one another gently and affectionately, and seem to be supportive without ostentatious acknowledgments. Their love flows out of them toward each other and the rest of the world. They also have passionate, deeply felt sex.

What is the condition of the heart when we talk about "making love"? It is the very physical experience of warmth, fullness, and a feeling of supreme openness.

A couple with a thriving heart dimension possess a willingness to be

▶ Courageous

▶ Forgiving

▶ Healing

▶ Receiving

Don't we all want that? Wouldn't you always want to be in "easy love" with your partner? The passion created by a charged heart dimension enhances the love of two people who understand each other and have a tangible, loving commitment. The challenge is keeping the flame of this commitment alive, amidst or in spite of natural and realistic disappointments, anger, and hurt.

The core of the heart dimension is consciously tending and nurturing our love for our partner, and making that commitment feel vital, light, and easy. If our heart is open and generous toward our partner, we feel close, in sync, and in love. Making a transition from the first three physical dimensions—the biologic, sensual, and desire dimensions—to the heart and then the intimacy dimensions is a skill for all lovers to learn. It is the animal energy of the first dimensions that gives power and intensity to the more subtle essence of these next two dimensions, the heart and the intimacy, which are rooted in our emotions. Once our emotions become involved, we begin give our sexual connection meaning and permanence.

MAKING THE HEART TANGIBLE

But what is this heart connection we so casually talk about? Is it just a poetic term for caring for someone or is it real? As a doctor, I was taught to think first of the heart as an organ—the organ in charge of pumping the blood necessary for life throughout the body. Literally, the heart makes sure that the body receives all its vital oxygen and nutrients via the blood. Of course, without the heart, we die. When the heart is weak or ill (as in the case after a heart attack or with someone suffering from heart disease), it doesn't work as well or as strongly, and this subpar performance affects our entire body's function.

Recently some interesting studies have gone beyond seeing the heart as a pump to look at the connection between the heart and the brain via our nervous system. It has been discovered and clearly delineated that our heart is governed millisecond to millisecond by an exquisite balance in the autonomic nervous system. One side of this nervous system, the sympathetic, charges us and gets us ready for "fight or flight." It increases the heart rate and sends massive amounts of blood to the lungs for oxygenation and then feeds the large muscles of our body. The other half of this nervous system, the parasympathetic, is in control when we are calm and relaxed, when we are enjoying each other's company without stress or emotional strain. Interestingly, in our society, many events—such as traffic snarls, problems at the office, arguments with children—can repeatedly push us into sympathetic dominance. Since this system is really designed for emergency use only, this can have a bad effect on our health. In effect, we are always "in an emergency."

When our body is constantly stressed, we are at increased risk for abnormal electrical beats of our heart, or arrythmias. In fact, men and women who have an imbalance in the sympathetic/parasympathetic system are at high risk for sudden death. They flood their hearts with adrenaline over and over.

Researchers at the Institute of Heart Math have investigated this relationship quite closely and have made a fascinating discovery. They have found that when individuals are asked to simply focus on their heart, much as you might focus on your knee or your toe, and to begin to recall in detail an experience of pleasure, happiness, or feeling loved, the balance between the sympathetic and parasympathetic systems is restored. Voilà! It can be as quick as that!

The heart rate variability, which reflects this balance of the two systems, is increased and augmented when this heartfelt connection is made. Literally, we have enhanced physiologic function when we are "in our hearts."

This data has convinced me that making this heartfelt connection with another human being is not an abstract or romantic concept, but rather an actual physiologic event that denotes optimal functioning of the human organism. In fact, researchers have measured the electromagnetic force of the heart as far as ten feet away from the body! This is not an "aura" or some imaginary substance but an actual field that denotes the powerful energy of the heart, which is sixty times stronger than brain waves. The trick, of course, is for all of us to augment this heart energy and bring connection and commitment into our lovemaking. Using this metaphor, imagine your heart and that of your partner. Concentrate on sending out a calm, loving current. Open your heart and let the connection flow through. When your heart is balanced and feels appreciated, you will literally be in sync with your partner.

THE FOUR-CHAMBERED HEART

As I've developed the concept of the multidimensional sexual relationship over the past ten years, I've found the more concretely we think of our feelings, especially about sex, the more likely we are to have wonderful, fantastic lovemaking. As I've suggested before, the best way to infuse energy into your heart connection with your partner is to think of your heart (love) as a living, breathing entity.

The heart in its anatomical form has four chambers. These four chambers have helped me to focus on the positive aspects of this dimension. To have a generous, full, large heart, we need to have the elements of courage, forgiveness, healing, and the ability to receive. These four characteristics correspond to the four chambers of the human heart and are the necessary elements for a heartfelt connection during sex with your partner.

COURAGE

It is no coincidence that the word *courage* comes from the French word *coeur,* which means "heart." Indeed, to have a real, deep heart connection it is first necessary to risk vulnerability, which requires courage. When you reach out to your lover, it takes courage; when you extend your heart energy, it takes courage; and when you are open to what you will receive, it takes courage.

Clarissa Pinkola Estes in her book *Women Who Run with the Wolves* describes the myth of Bluebeard, an extremely handsome, powerful man with a beard so black, it appears blue. Madly in love with a young maiden, he woos the girl until she agrees to marry him. Once married, Bluebeard takes his new bride home, where he gives her the run of the entire mansion. But with one warning: Never go into the cellar. After a couple of idyllic years, she cannot resist the temptation and steals a small key to gain access to the cellar. She there discovers the disintegrating bodies of all of Bluebeard's previous wives. Knowing that he will now have to kill her too, she enlists the help of her sisters and flees into the woods, narrowly escaping his wrath.

This myth expresses the emotions and fears that all of us encounter as we begin to love one another and become vulnerable. We risk finding out things about ourselves and our lovers that take us out of the idyllic, naive space that we often associate with or think of as "falling or being in love." We discover the cellar and experience the shock of a cruel and unforgiving heart. It is one thing to fall in love the first time and then be disappointed because we had no idea how bad it could be. It is a much different act of trust, faith, and courage to risk falling in love again and again, knowing the cellar exists, knowing how it hurts to be disappointed and, at times, even devastated. The man or woman who decides to open his or her heart again has undeniable courage.

FORGIVENESS

The forgiveness chamber is what often keeps us from whole-hearted sex, and its Achilles' heel is anger. Though anger runs through all the dimensions, here in the heart dimension, it actually has the ability to close down the heart forever. This anger can be directed either at yourself or at your partner. Sometimes, there is residual anger at someone else (for instance, a parent or an old lover). Yet difficult as it may be to set anger aside, I have found that the ability to forgive is absolutely necessary for the heart to be open and stay open.

There is a great Zen story about a famous warrior who, after proving himself awesome in battle again and again, was finally wounded by an arrow, which pierced his body beneath his armor. Angered at his vulnerability and at his attacker, he vowed not to remove the arrow until he found the man who had released it in battle. A month later, the great warrior died of a smoldering but invasive infection. The Zen masters pose this question: Who killed the mighty warrior? The man who shot the arrow, or the man who refused to pull the arrow out?

As you have probably guessed, it was the warrior himself who was the real assailant. In his stubbornness and anger (some may call this vengeance), he destroyed his own heart. It is often stubbornness or pride that makes us cling to our anger, but more often than not what keeps the anger alive, what fuels it, is a hurt we have not allowed to heal. Carrying around anger is like nurturing an abscess in our own heart; righteous though we may be, it is poisonous to ourself. Letting go of anger means also letting go of the satisfaction of revenge and truly accepting the pain of our hurt.

Over the years that I have been doing sexual counseling, one thing has become abundantly clear to me: You cannot make love to someone you hate!

You can have sex of course. Plenty of physical connection can be experienced in the sexual realm. But to have the desire to *make love,* there must be access to the emotional territory, a space that cannot be walled off! Often our anger becomes a treasure, a medal of a war, maybe even one of the major reasons for our existence. We can grow to love our wounds as keepsakes and keep them close to our chest, polishing them from time to time, and dragging them out when we are backed into a corner. "Oh, so you didn't appreciate the way I treated you at the market yesterday? Well, remember the time you . . ." And we launch into a well-rehearsed recital of past injustices, feeling ever so righteous. However, this treasure chest of anger becomes an impossibly heavy burden around the neck of desire.

A telling story of treasured anger that destroyed the heart connection occurred many years ago in my practice during a sexual-enhancement class for women. Two weeks into the program, Beth began to share something about her situation. Quietly, she revealed that three years ago her husband had had an affair.

"Who did he have the affair with?" I asked.

"My best friend." The words dropped heavily into the group. Beth added, "I was the last person to find out. Everyone else knew about it."

I asked Beth how she had discovered the affair, and she reported that she had intercepted a letter of his to his lover. All of the details were in that letter. Beth went on to say that she still had the letter.

"You still have it?" I said.

"Yes, I have it with me, in my purse."

"Why?" I could not help blurting out.

"Because if I leave it at home, Steve might find it. And if he finds it, he might destroy it. And if I decide to divorce him, I'm going to need the letter to get custody of the kids."

It was clear there was a problem. Beth was in this class to improve her sexual relationship with her husband, yet she had the letter in her purse! That letter was a treasure that she carried everywhere. In fact, it was as important as her wallet; after three years it had become a permanent symbol of her broken heart.

Now, don't get me wrong. Beth certainly had a right to be angry. It was a dirty, stinky thing that Steve had done. But, remember, you can't make love to someone you hate. Since Beth wanted to stay with Steve, wanted to have exceptional sex with him, she had to confront her deep anger and feelings of betrayal toward Steve before she was going to have the heart to bring him into her body during lovemaking. Otherwise she was going to continue to tolerate sex as a detached, impersonal act at best.

Two years later I happened to see Beth again. She was walking down the soccer field after her son's team had played my son's team. She was arm in arm with a man, her face beaming with a big smile. My mind raced: "Is this a new man or is this her husband, Steve?" She came up and introduced me to Steve, saying that with professional help they had been able to work everything out and were now happier than ever. I walked away amazed and actually delighted that they were so obviously connected. Somehow she had been able to let go of the letter and reopen her heart. And, I presume, Steve was able to make a genuine heart commitment to her.

Clearly, it was not and is not my job to tell Beth and others with understandable hurt and anger what to do. That is an individual decision. Equally clear is that you must address your grievances against each other before you can open the interior spaces of the heart and soul.

How to forgive, however, is a skill that can be learned. Like any skill, it requires practice, and obviously some things are easier to forgive than others. You don't have to be a saint to forgive. Everyone can do it—make the process and the practice of the skill concrete. Sometimes (i.e., some days) it's easier than others, and forgiveness hinges on the ability to see that usually the injury has predecessors. Some old sore from childhood or an earlier vulnerable time is reopened by a comment, glance, or action. I can think of several such incidents involving me and my husband. David may know that he is not being particularly kind, but it is my reaction over which I have control. As I see that it is usually his hurt, exhaustion, or frustration that is being expressed, the wound becomes less about me and more about him and is much easier to forgive! Also, I have learned that forgiveness takes space and time. I may need to take a walk, go into the garden, think a bit before I react. These actions give me back my perspective, allow me to remind myself that we have a great love between us that is being jostled. As we will discuss in the intimacy dimension, I do not advocate forgiving cruel behavior, physical or emotional, nor do I think one person has to do all the forgiving. There must be mutuality and respect in all the dimensions of sex, especially so in the heart.

In my experience, *self-forgiveness* is one of the most important and most difficult achievements. There is the continuous inner voice that points out deficiencies and mistakes and shrivels our heart with judgment and condemnation. In this way, we are, in a sense, abandoning our own heart. So the next chamber of the generous heart has to do with healing, ourselves *and* our partner.

HEALING

The ability to heal with heart energy is also extremely important to maintaining an open heart connection with your partner. Healing revolves around succor. Succor is our ability to acknowledge the pain and hurt of another and choose to extend our energy to heal this person.

In Tantra, there is a wonderful and sweet exercise called a healing massage (taught in chapter 9), wherein one partner begins to stimulate the other, giving sensual pleasure to and arousing the other person without making any demands on him or her. Intercourse, no matter how tempting, is strictly forbidden so that the exchange goes only one way, from the healer to the person receiving. Although this exercise may sound simple, it is actually an elegant and challenging approach to addressing some of the wounds that we all have, especially where sexuality is concerned.

Opening one's heart, having an intimate connection, allows this healing of old and sometimes deep wounds to progress. Laurie and George were not sure what exactly had changed in their relationship. George described their sexual connection as nourishing, but he came to see me to explore what more was available to him and Laurie sexually. Laurie, on the other hand, presented a different story. Over the past year she had experienced a sharp decline in her sexual interest. Although she could still lubricate and have orgasms, she did not feel the passion she was accustomed to in her interaction with George. As she began to pinpoint when this change occurred, she realized that her feelings had shifted at the time of her father's death.

Laurie and her father had always had a special relationship. They talked often, they respected each other a great deal, and their love was deep. Laurie felt a terrible void after he died, and though it made no sense to her, she began to feel as if it were inappropriate for her to be sensual, erotic, or sexual. Her father had never had a prudish attitude toward sex and would certainly not expect that of Laurie. However, Laurie's loss prevented her from accessing the sexual joy and energy that she was accustomed to.

Thankfully, after our discussion, George clearly recognized that Laurie's loss had made her more needy, and he began to show his love and commitment to her in more obvious ways. He began to approach her more tenderly and to utilize the healing massage to connect with her body while he was mending her heart. As time went on, Laurie could both laugh and cry when they were connected heart to heart during their lovemaking. She naturally recovered her lustful self as her grief lessened and her heart healed. George, rather than experiencing emotional distance from Laurie, was pleased that he could be part of her recovery of passion. George's ability to provide succor and reach out to her in a healing spirit not only helped Laurie process her grief, but also enriched their sexual connection. Sex became a vehicle for healing.

RECEIVING

Finally, the last chamber of the heart is the ability to receive. Even if you continually extend yourself to others, even in forgiveness or with courage or with the intent to heal, you will be unable to fully experience the sexual heart dimension unless the exchange goes both ways. Many individuals protect themselves by always giving and never allowing themselves to be vulnerable enough to receive. Renee was a bright, bubbly young woman who loved to talk. She was funny, charming, and perceptive. I watched her make friends quickly and easily in the couples group. Her husband, John, was tall and good-looking. He also had an easy smile and a sense of earnestness. At first glance, the two of them seemed to be without any issues. But as Renee began to confront the "homework" of receiving a sexual pleasuring session from John, she showed signs of the trouble that had plagued her.

In our discussion, she said that in the four years she and John had been together, John had sometimes wanted to have really slow sex. When other women in the group looked at her with envy, she proclaimed, "I hated it!" She would then tell him, "Let's get going. We need to go for it." Renee explained that she didn't want to "waste time" with too much foreplay, and she definitely did not like the idea of looking into John's eyes.

Curious, I asked Renee to tell me more.

"Oh," she said, "I just like sex for sex. It's fun to go for the orgasm and then I'm done. That's how I have been since a teenager. I always hear about women talking about how they got such bad messages from their mothers about sex, and mine was just the opposite. She had me when she was seventeen, and when I was growing up, there was a string of men that came and went in and out of our lives."

Renee continued somewhat sarcastically, "I knew none of them really loved Mom, but she was just exploring her own sexuality I guess."

I suspected that the breeziness in Renee's voice belied what it must have been like for a young girl to have to deal with her young mother's multiple sexual partners. Renee observed that it had taken a couple of years of counseling to come to terms with her mother's actions.

John chimed in that he felt that Renee had never shown him the "real" her. He said that although he thoroughly enjoyed their hot and fun sex, he often didn't feel connected to her. After sex, he would always wonder if she truly loved him. He wanted more and told Renee so.

Renee knew intellectually what he was expressing. She even knew that she really did not trust men after what she had seen with her mother, but when John began being earnest about their lovemaking, she started detaching. She was observant enough of herself to see that during the more intensely loving nonsexual exercises in our workshop, she would begin looking intently at her nails or examining her hair for split ends or complaining that it was too hot in the room or that the wrong music was playing. *Anything* to avoid opening up to *receive* from her husband. Receiving meant letting John into her inner, closely guarded heart; receiving meant becoming vulnerable to rejection; receiving meant surrendering power.

Although Renee and John did not turn this pattern around with one or two conversations and homework assignments, after the workshop they both understood the value to their sexual joy of a true heart connection. Renee's self-honesty kept her working on this issue, even though it was scary for her, because she understood that sex without heart was empty, and that giving without receiving undermines your partner's value.

The four-chambered heart beats throughout our lives—sometimes vigorously, and sometimes with little energy. This cycle or pattern of change is natural. What couples need to think about and focus on is how to sustain the heart's strength.

As your relationship's most vital organ, it needs to be treated with constant care, respect, and love.

Early in relationships, it is easy to feel open and generous with our love. But later, as time passes, we often begin to tally hurts, angers, or wounds, and the tokens and gifts mean less and less, the anniversaries feel like more of an obligation. Without fully realizing what we are doing, we are erecting emotional walls between ourself and our partner. The bricks of this wall are made up of the harsh words directed at one another: the missed birthday or anniversary, the casual or not so casual disappointments with one another. Slowly, gradually, our brick wall becomes mortared with the cement of bitterness so that our heart is closed, hard, *and* stingy. We are cut off from our own feelings of love and begin to feel isolated or distant from our partner. Who laid down that first brick? What angry reaction or jealous feeling or deep hurt made us emotionally or physically step away from our partner, paving the way for the barrier to be constructed?

These walls are different for each person and each couple, but all of them are difficult to tear down once construction has begun in earnest. Some hurts or withdrawals are not necessarily irrevocable and are often natural blips or bumps that can be crossed or ignored easily. But how many of us have let hurt or anger create a gulf that seems unbridgeable, a barrier that feels impenetrable?

I believe that a wonderful, ever-expanding heart connection is not only possible throughout a relationship but that it is absolutely necessary for our sexual happiness. Indeed, the heart is the wellspring of our most vital connection to our partner. It is the source that provides the sustenance for a long-term loving, sexual relationship. If the heart is not engaged, if that connection is not tended to and strengthened, a relationship will die—even if there are other strong aspects of the connection. A couple may share many great qualities, including a social or financial bond, good friendships, or even strong sexual attraction or lust. But if they don't have a powerful heart connection, sooner or later their relationship will begin to wither. So how do we nurture this flame? What puts it out?

THE STINGY HEART

Many of us have had enough experiences with abandonment or disappointment that we no longer feel generous of heart. Or, we may be able to express one or two aspects of the committed and generous heart only some of the time. And yet, we have not actually abandoned the relationship. Instead, we move into that passive middle space where we are not fully committed to our partner either sexually or sensually with the fullness of our being. Rather, we exist in the stagnant space of the stingy heart. A major indication that your heart dimension may be weak or suffering in your relationship is if you and/or your partner tend to withhold sex, as a way of withholding love.

The stingy heart is a shriveled heart. Not only does it not speak poetically or romantically, it also restricts itself from speaking or feeling at all. The stingy heart uses its energy to protect itself with many locks and keys. These locks keep it closed and unable to let in or let out feeling.

But we are not always aware that our heart has become stingy. One patient of mine, Janelle, had always thought of herself as openhearted. She gave kisses and hugs to show her love; she took time to send cards, make gifts. Yet when she and her husband, Tom, came to the couples workshop, Janelle was blown away by the realization that a large part of her heart was locked away from her husband. Janelle came to see that emotionally she was largely going through the motions with Tom.

It was clear to me during the workshop that her heart shrank from his gaze. She discovered through the soul-gazing exercise (see the techniques section) that she actually needed to keep a part of her from him because she was so terrified of being abandoned. These fears had their roots in her childhood rather than in any early love relationships, but they governed the depth of her openness to Tom. In fact, his wide-open love for her created anxiety in her heart because that level of love put the ball back in her court. "Can I even begin to match his love for me? Can I play the game at this level?" were the questions Janelle was faced with. Her mind knew that Tom was not going to abandon her as members of her family had done, but her heart had to believe this also. The small, terrified child who had closed the doors to her heart long ago now had to identify the courage, receiving, and healing chambers. Her initial wide-eyed, slightly startled look softened over the next few days as she became more comfortable with Tom's loving, calm gaze. She began not only to understand but to feel how lonely and stingy her heart had been, how undernourished their lovemaking had been. Gradually she allowed more and more of the loving feelings in when they did their sexual homework; gradually she came to believe in her own full, vibrant heart.

Tom didn't have to have his wife completely change overnight. As far as he was concerned, it was a huge step in their relationship that Janelle could see what he had been feeling: her closed, careful, somewhat stingy heart.

At the end of the workshop, Tom gave Janelle what he called a "time capsule" of their love. It was a simple but beautifully crafted cylinder, not purchased but created, that represented a new beginning of a wide-open, heart-brimming sexual connection.

He fashioned this gift for both of them to look back on years hence. The capsule included tokens of their life together and heart-shaped stones to represent their renewed commitment. He also presented tissues for both of them for the tears of joy they had shed as he began to receive her heart energy fully for the first time. All of us in the workshop needed tissues after his presentation of that gift!

The stingy heart also keeps track of who gave what to whom and when and how long it's been. It is watchful and is usually tallying up a score sheet between both individuals. One couple came to me on the brink of separation. Alice and Mark had been married ten years and had four children under nine. They were both teachers, but Alice had stayed home raising their four kids. Needless to say, money was tight and tensions were high.

By the time they reached my office, Alice had moved into a guest bedroom, and even the thought of sex with Mark had become impossible. She felt hopeless, exhausted from the arguing and the heaviness of their relationship. I asked each of them to describe what they felt was wrong with their relationship. Alice began describing how she didn't get what she needed, and Mark did the same. I heard them loud and clear, describing what I call a tit-for-tat cycle.

They had become caught in a pattern of who does more for the kids. Since they both felt burdened by the responsibilities of caring for the children under the stress of a tight budget, they acted out their frustration and lack of control in their own relationship. Instead of sharing the responsibilities, the struggles, the internal pain, and letting their love bind them, they did the reverse. They became divided as a couple, competing for free time, and comparing who did more around the house, and for the children. This division undermined their commitment, and each of them had lost a tangible sense of their love for each other. How familiar! How easy it is to blame someone else for life's travails. How convenient, and how destructive.

What to do?

I have to be honest. I was not so sure I could help this couple. Their sense of love and commitment had eroded to such a degree, and the battle of wills they engaged in was so pervasive, that I was pessimistic. I was unsure that illuminating their destructive patterns, as well as pointing them in the direction of their past joy, and highlighting all the wonderful feelings that had drawn them together in the first place, would be enough to rekindle their thirst for love.

After much discussion of their history, their connection did improve greatly with insight. Both of them agreed that they needed a change in their habits of heart. But they were unable to stop blaming each other all of the time.

Remember, the stingy heart says, "I don't want to share or give up my toys. I am feeling demanding or withholding. I don't want to give *to* you because it feels like giving *in* to you. If I do something only for you, I might lose my autonomy, and I don't really want to commit to you because I am at risk for abandonment." The generous heart, on the other hand, shares because it will receive more in return, bestows forgiveness because it provides strength for the forgiver, risks receiving in order to exclude loneliness, and believes that love heals most wounds.

HOW ANGER SHRIVELS THE HEART

Being angry and getting hurt are aspects of everyday living. They are feelings we all have. The question is what do we do with these feelings. Once when I was in a particularly black mood and was seeking to blame my husband, I wrote this poem:

TRUE NATURE

Eyes narrowed and
heart constricted,
I look about to see
how to blame you.

It must be your fault
that I am not happy today.

Where are my flowers?
Why is there not enough money
for me to be
expansive,
extravagant,
my true nature?

Stuck on the thorns of anger
I wait for you to become
the silken pillow amid opulent gardens.

I resist the lesson of self-creation
preferring to sit,
wide bottomed,
on the stoic cushion
of disappointment—
my fingers wrapped around the mug
of steaming circumstance.

I sip its poison of powerless broth
and continue to die
inside out.

Whew! I still remember how I felt that day and how much I wanted to make my feelings his fault and something he should fix for me. Of course, it is the victim who dies from the inside out, I know that, but it is so tempting to blame the other person and to hold on to our injury. Why it is so difficult to let go of past hurts, to give up these treasured wounds? One reason is that we believe if we do, the other person will have gotten away with something. Another reason is that we believe if we give up the hurt, it means that the injury was somehow insignificant. We know that it was important and therefore we must continue to acknowledge the scar.

If it is a major wound or betrayal, such as an affair, or if the anger has been simmering for years and is a major part of your dynamic as a couple, you will want professional counseling. But even when the issues appear trivial in the larger scheme of life, small bitter heart treasures need to be addressed, because if they aren't, they will form a poisonous backdrop to any attempt at open, ecstatic lovemaking.

Ted and Norma came in to discuss their lack of sexual con- nection. Ted complained that Norma rejected most of his attempts to initiate sex, and Norma admitted that it was true. Because they began by speaking about problems with initiating sex, I thought at first that they were having trouble in the desire or lust dimension. But the more I listened to Norma and Ted, the more I heard another story.

Norma said she felt empty when she made love. She also said that she was afraid of Ted. Afraid? How so? Norma indi- cated that Ted was always angry. He was mad at the grocery clerk, furious with the traffic, snarling at the waitress, demean- ing to the children. Everything fired him up. He had an angry, irritable style that had unfortunately often allowed him to get his way just because others wanted him out of their face.

Although Ted was not often openly hostile with Norma, she was always trying to modulate his angry tirades or to ignore their effect on those around them.

As she spoke, Ted slouched down in his chair. Finally he admitted it was all true, but what could he do? The world was full of imbeciles and infuriating situations.

Ted had an anger habit. Anger fueled him, it got him up in the morning, it stimulated him, it released the tension of not getting his way; he couldn't imagine life without it. He could see some of the effects it had on Norma, but he had no idea that it had prevented her from making love to him. As we discussed the idea that "feelings are facts," Ted admitted that it made sense that Norma could not open her heart to him when he was raging.

What to do? I gave Ted the hardest assignment of his life: he was to go one entire day without being angry! He sputtered, he protested, he said it would be impossible because of the idiots he was always encountering, but he agreed to try.

When I talked to Ted a couple of days later, he reported that he had a difficult time discarding what I called his anger habit. But he was able to see how pervasive it was simply by realizing how difficult it was to give up. He began to understand the damage he was doing not only to his relationship but also to his own body. Norma was so happy that he was trying to change that she was willing to cut him some slack. She saw the vulnerable man underneath the anger and was anxious to open her heart to him. With her support, he began to change his destructive pattern.

To let go of anger, hurt, or disappointment is an act of will. It is also often an act of courage and of hope for the future. It may be an act of forgiveness of ourself or another. All of us can get comfortable on our cushions of disappointment, but they are lonely perches, especially when what we really want to do is dance. If we are ready to move on to a better future, we may be able to say to our partner, "Remember the time you . . . ? I would like it if you could say you are sorry one more time. But even if you don't, I have decided to give up that hurt. I will never speak of it again." (I strongly believe that the person who holds the anger actually suffers more than the one who occasionally gets it.)

And then you give it up. Forever. Period. When thoughts of the old hurt occur again, you say to yourself, "Oh, there is that old wound again. I'm not putting any more energy into it. I am going to think of something else." If you have been in the habit of treasuring these slights, this behavior will require some vigilance, but the payoff will be palpable relief and a much greater access to joy.

FEAR OF ABANDONMENT

A major threat that can shake the ground of commitment (the root of our heart dimension) is fear of abandonment. Let's face it, all of us have had an experience of physical or emotional abandonment as a child or in an early love relationship. We were heartbroken, we had heartache, we swore never again to have our heart on our sleeve, we sang along with every country-western song! As a result, our heart became wary and hardened by that early experience. We avoid making a commitment again, not wanting to risk the hurt and pain. In fact, some of us become so intent (either consciously or unconsciously) on avoiding abandonment, we simply don't make a heart commitment in the first place. This push-pull dance between men and women is due to the fear of opening up and receiving. Being open can feel dangerously close to the cliff of abandonment.

I have often observed how the fear of "being left again" can create a powerful legacy in a relationship. As most of us do, Peggy and Paul got together with some emotional baggage. Before meeting Peggy, Paul had given up on marriage after his first wife, whom he loved deeply, had had an affair that ultimately resulted in a painful divorce. Needless to say, Paul was shattered, and determined never to let himself be that vulnerable again. In fact, he had several years of superficial relationships where he had a "great time" and during which his main goal was not to be tied down.

Peggy's history was also marked by abandonment. As a child, her life had been disrupted by her mother's drug addiction and ultimate suicide. Now Peggy was an extremely cautious adult, tentative about becoming close to anyone.

Despite the odds, when Paul and Peggy met, they were both immediately struck by an intense attraction. Suddenly Paul said he was ready for intimacy and commitment to Peggy. At the same time, Peggy described knowing right at the beginning that Paul was the one, telling me that she had found herself saying "I love you" early in their relationship.

Soon after their marriage, Peggy complained that sometimes when they were making love, she would "leave the scene," becoming distracted. Like a punctured balloon, the wonderful energy between them would dissipate. As we discussed her experience of lovemaking with Paul, Peggy realized that she had spent much of her life avoiding emotional intensity because of the chaos of her early home life. When she encountered intensity, her learned response was to flee the scene.

As Peggy became aware of the roots of this pattern, she was able to lock eyes with Paul during those moments of fear and begin to tolerate the intensity of their connection. On Paul's part, he battled against his fearful response to Peggy's temporary withdrawals. I advised them to work on creating a container of safety in which they both would feel comfortable exploring the entire range of their love for one another. This container was physically manifested by Peggy and Paul's sitting on their bed facing each other and holding hands. As they looked into the other's eyes quietly, the space between them filled with emotional warmth and deep caring. When the energy of this eye-to-eye connection threatened to become overwhelming, each had permission to close his or her eyes briefly, to go inside to be reminded of the quiet strength each had developed individually, and then to reopen to the visual connection. Day after day they practiced creating this chalice of safety and love and were often surprised at the sexual desire that arose during these quiet moments. They learned that they could weather times of fear and minor detachments and still remain connected and committed. Peggy and Paul were determined to have a vibrant relationship with extraordinary sex, and they were learning that that meant their sexual connection had to have heart.

EMPTY SYMBOLS, FALSE GESTURES

Often, our automatic association with the heart is romance. When we first think of love, we think of images of curling up together before a roaring fire, eating with our lover bathed in candlelight, or being met at the door with a dozen long-stemmed roses. These are a few of the many images that we associate with the heart, which we in turn connect with love. Often we use such images to imagine feeling warm and loving toward our partner. It's as if without such triggers, we don't believe we'll "get there," to that place of spontaneous, open-hearted love. We use romantic symbols as conduits for our tender feelings that we otherwise save for special occasions or believe only existed in the so-called honeymoon stage of our relationship. And while gifts and symbolic gestures can be powerful expressions of feeling that mean a great deal to us or our loved one, they can also be misused or overused, replacing real, palpable contact. We all know that having sex without heart is a very different experience, one that can be empty. We end up feeling as if we are being serviced rather than being loved.

Women tend to be more aware of the value and power of commitment and love and therefore are often more fluent in its language. For example, in a relationship it is often the woman who is the keeper of the dates, the planner of romance, the thoughtful one. Women use the totems of love, such as cards, poetry, gifts, and wedding rings, as symbols of romance and solidarity—ways of saying not only "I love you" but also "I am yours and you are mine." And they expect to receive these same symbolic totems as important and powerful signs of love and affection from their partner or mate. When these gifts are not received, women often question the depth or level of their man's commitment.

Women feel that they are supposed to be wooed and won by romantic signs of love, and most men dutifully cooperate with these customs of the heart but often feel nowhere near the emotional investment in this concept that women do. Some men choke on the words "I love you," so reluctant are they to use such a powerful term. Others say it almost casually, leaving the listener to wonder what the declaration of "love" actually means.

The heart dimension is often sentimentalized and pandered to by the marketing industry, which insists on telling us how we should be feeling and what we should be getting and giving. This results in what I call bogus gift-giving, where the action of giving a gift is really a manipulation or an empty gesture. Either the giver wants something in return for the gift or merely wants the gift to replace the demand to really communicate his or her feelings. Things may look good (even feel good) on the outside, but lurking behind the facade might be a questioning, aching heart in need of real love.

Faye had more than enough "stuff," as she called it. She lived in a beautiful house in a lovely part of town, she had more jewelry than she could wear, and she even got huge bouquets of flowers on her birthday and on her anniversary. But she didn't feel that she had Bud's attention. Faye was not convinced that he had opened his heart to her.

However, Bud was resolute in his declaration of love for Faye. He had heard her complaints many times, and they had even had many discussions with other counselors about this issue.

When given the assignment in the couples workshop to find or make a gift for Faye (he was forbidden to buy anything because that was too easy for a man of means), he took the task seriously. Throughout several days, he scanned his environment for something and finally discovered a beautiful rock with many colors, veins, and surfaces. As he presented this to Faye, he eloquently described his emotional connection to her. Each little crevice had meaning, each color reflected something between the two of them.

During the days of searching for his gift for Faye, he had also become aware of the heart that he kept so protected and hidden. He made the connection between the loss of a parent when he was a child as well as other losses in his life and his fear of abandonment. Faye loved this small rock because it was a real gift, given with thought, love, and an open, generous heart. To her, it meant much more than her jewelry or fancy car: it was a simple yet vivid sign of her husband's love and commitment. It represented his willingness to make a heart-to-heart connection.

It's not always easy to give a real gift to the person you love, and it's easy to buy into the material nature of our culture, in which we are constantly reminded of "things" we need or should have. However, I have found that those couples who express their love with actions, gestures, or tokens that are thoughtful and tied straight to the heart have a keener sense of energy in this dimension.

TECHNIQUES FOR STRENGTHENING YOUR HEART CONNECTION

Here are some suggestions for opening and strengthening your own heart connection.

1. HEART AWARENESS

Each day, at least once a day, practice becoming aware of your heart. See if you can imagine it beating in your chest, sending out a large force field. Then remember an occasion when you felt touched in a heartfelt way. Perhaps you recall playing with a child, tussling with your dog, sitting on your grandparents' porch, experiencing a fabulous sunset. Bring back the sensations in all the sensory detail that you can manage, and let the imagery open your heart. This practice, which is a part of the freeze-frame technique developed by the Heart Math folks, not only changes your physiology, it provides the experience of what it feels like to have an open heart. When you have practiced a bit, imagine thinking of something that chills you and closes your heart, and then notice how that feels.

The third step is to hold your partner's hands and do first the open-heart imagery and then the one of the closed heart. See if your partner can feel the difference. You can always ask your partner to do the same and try to guess which state he or she is in. I bet that you will be right!

2. SOUL GAZING

This is a crucial tool of the heart dimension that comes from the Tantra tradition we will discuss in the transpersonal dimension. It builds on the open heart exercise you have just read about. In this case you and your partner are making a connection to construct a container for making love. First, you sit across from one another and hold hands. The left hand of both partners is held palm up to represent receiving (remember, receiving is a chamber of the generous heart), and the right hand is placed palm down on your partner's hand to represent giving. Next, you begin looking in one another's eyes. And don't talk! You'll talk about money or the kids! To silently look into the eyes of your lover takes courage, one of the heart's chambers as we've mentioned, and it may feel as if you are being seen as never before. It may make you feel more naked than you have ever been, but because of this intensity, there is great power in this simple exercise. See if you can do this with an open heart. You can use your imagery from the first exercise to send your lover heart energy through your right hand to his or her heart. Begin to breathe together, slowly and easily. Generally the man has to follow his woman's breath because we have smaller lung capacity. Soon you will be synchronized and feeling a wonderful, focused connection. After just a few minutes of sending and receiving loving, open feelings, it is incredibly easy to reach out and touch your lover's body. You will learn a second level to this soul gazing later in the aesthetic dimension, but begin to practice this wonderful, transformative technique right away.

3. STINGY HEART SURVEILLANCE

If you have trouble with either of the first two tools, search your heart for anger. Something in your past may have shriveled your heart. The stingy heart does not want to open, it does not want to let anyone else in, and it certainly does not want to give or forgive. If your eyes dart around the room instead of looking into your beloved's, or if you have to force them to remain on your partner's face, a part of you probably feels anxious about the heart connection. Do not judge yourself too harshly, just notice this feeling and become curious about the cause. If your partner has this trouble, ask if this is difficult for him or her. Become curious about why, ask how it feels, say "Tell me more," and be careful not to take your partner's difficulty onto yourself. There may indeed be issues that have to be resolved between the two of you, but only your partner can open his or her heart for the powerful business of receiving and giving.

4. CONSCIOUS KISSING

Develop the skill of the conscious kiss. Use your skills from the sensual dimension to become an expert kisser. Now, in the morning or evening, when you are kissing hello or good-bye, make it a real kiss, one from the heart. Take that extra minute to soften your lips, to notice the heat of your partner's mouth, to dance tongues, and to draw his or her delicate skin into your mouth. Whew! That will make greeting and leave-taking a new experience that will permeate the mundane, daily routine. Conscious kissing is so easy to incorporate for most of us if we merely remember to do it. It keeps the heart channel open.

5. SEXUAL HEART HEALING

Become an expert at using the heart focus to heal. This final chamber of the generous heart is powerful. As Teilhard de Chardin said, "Man will learn to harness the power of love, and for the second time in the history of mankind we will have discovered fire." When you have reins on the power of love, you can direct it to whoever needs healing. Bestowing love during sex is even more astounding because we are often open and vulnerable at that time. When we are about to climax and our partner murmurs, "You are so beautiful, I love you so much," it is as if the world opens up to receive us. There we become whole.

6. HEART LISTS

Exchange a "heart list" with your lover, five things that your partner could do that would open your heart. To do this you have to discard the notion that "if I have to tell them to do it, then it doesn't count." We all love to be surprised by the tokens of this dimension. It may be a love poem, written on a piece of scratch paper during a business flight away from your honey; it might be a funny, sentimental card, or a single rose. It could be playing his or her type of music while making love even if it is not your favorite sound. Especially if you or your partner have suffered significant abandonment, many little reminders of your connection create a feeling of security and commitment.

7. JUST FOR YOU

Finally, perhaps you will want to change something that you do that you know is annoying. There are always little habits that annoy our beloved, even though we don't think that they really matter. In fact, we think that our loved one is being picky or obsessive or nagging about whatever it is. However, changing our pattern just for our partner is a generous gesture and goes a long way to open his or her heart. Watch those couples who extend the generous heart toward one another, and take from them the innumerable small ways they keep the heart channel open.

AN OPEN HEART IS A GENEROUS HEART

How can we blend sex and love, lust and love, getting it on and getting in touch? By consciously connecting our heart to our pelvis, believing that each blesses the other with its unique life force. When we risk discarding our fear of abandonment, when we let someone see both our sexual desire and capacity to love, when we refuse to have a stingy heart, we open up all of the power and strength of commitment and generosity. The heart dimension is the arena where lovers use the energy of the first three dimensions—the health of the biologic, the power of the desire, and the pleasure of the sensual—to connect to their own and their partner's emotions. In this way, the heart dimension is critical for achieving magnificent, multidimensional loving.

Learning how to have sex with an open heart can be difficult and complicated, especially when one or both of you are
wounded or withdrawn. The key is to approach loving as if it
were as concrete an act as intercourse. Since most of us think of
love as an abstract concept, we may not realize that love is not
only emotional, it's also physical. When you actually feel the
heart opening up, there is such an intense connection with your
partner that you will want to linger in this place.

But it does require practice; the more you do connect the
heart and the genitals, the more subtle your experience and
awareness will be. Imagine the practice of opening your heart as
if you were training for a sport: each time you practice (using
the exercises above), you increase your focus and quality of
attention, you enhance your skill, you get to know the strengths
of your teammate, all of which will then change your own
game, making it more intensely pleasurable.

The heart dimension is pivotal, for unless this channel of
love is truly open between two people, all the hot sex, and all the
words, gifts, and intentions in the world, won't connect you—it
just won't be or feel real. The goal of this game is to feel and
experience the heart connection as a concrete, palpable flow in
the powerful sexual river.

As you will see in the next chapter, on the intimacy dimension, with each successive dimension we take the energy built
from these connections to even higher levels of human sexual
communication. Our next aspect of lovemaking focuses on the
truth and sex.

6

A Fertile Garden, a Rich Tapestry

BUILDING DEPTH IN THE INTIMACY DIMENSION

TRUTH

Truth and Falsehood were bathing.

Falsehood came out of the water first
And dressed herself in Truth's clothing.

Truth,
Unwilling to put on the garments of Falsehood,
Went naked.

—ANONYMOUS

THE GREATEST GIFT

Remember when you first got to know your lover? You probably spent hours talking, getting to know everything about the other person. It was exhilarating, exciting, and erotic. The energy of first meeting and *really* getting to know another person can feel like receiving an intriguing, never-ending present: before learning how to enjoy the gift, we must open or unwrap the package to find out what is inside. How did this man or woman come to be? What does she think about this or that? What was her childhood like? What are her favorite things to do? To read? To see? Does she like the seaside or the mountains? Coffee or cola? How are we similar? How are we different?

Simultaneously with this mind-tingling curiosity about our new lover, we are also brimming with the desire to share information about ourself. We want this wonderful person to know us, the real, authentic us. *Because this is whom we want them to love.* As we take our first tentative and excited steps to forge a bond with a new lover, we risk allowing the truth about ourself to emerge. And despite our fear that what we are risking may bring about our rejection, we forge ahead, believing in the promise of the truth.

The truth about who we really are gives a relationship, specifically in the sexual arena, its distinct flavor, character, and intensity. Without the spiciness and texture of our uniqueness as men and women, the connection between you and your lover might be nourishing, but it would be bland. Without the charge that comes from revealing our true selves, a relationship would be safe, but not stimulating. Think of it this way: Our pets, especially dogs, give us a lot of heart energy. They are attentive, forgiving, even courageous, and certainly bring joy to our lives. But while they give us comfort, they don't surprise us with their complexity, intrigue us with their passions, make us work for the information that will help to seal our bond.

Whereas in the heart dimension we focused on making our sexual connection more loving and committed, in the intimacy dimension we focus on making the connection more intense by sharing and communicating with our partner from our most intimate place.

An intimacy dimension that is positively charged is based on trust and open communication. When these two essential factors are in place, your sexual relationship will deepen, involving you at the very core of your being. Truthful lovemaking is natural, spontaneous, and without guile. There is no reason to hide your lust or love or sensual expertise because all of you is available during sex. Deep honesty carries us to higher sex because we do not waste energy hiding or telling lies. It is as if you have taken your closest, most honest friendship and infused it with the spark of desire. The joy, laughter, humor, and playfulness are released with the freedom of letting go of caution and suspicion. You can dance the tango naked except for scarves, you can have tears on your breasts from sharing the truth while making love, you can let strength and vulnerability lie side by side while you are in your lover's arms.

Those couples who have developed a vital intimacy dimension share these qualities:

- They want to know the truth about each other—at all levels.
- They speak truthfully in their communication, avoiding outright lying and crafty withholding.
- They continue to share their personal aspirations with each other.
- They challenge and support each other in new endeavors.
- They talk frankly about what they like and want in their lovemaking.
- They share a sense of humor.
- They value and make time for emotional intimacy.

When these qualities are nurtured in a relationship, sex takes on another, deeper level of meaning. In the intimacy dimension, we focus on revealing and sharing our true, authentic selves. Specifically, when you and your partner are willing to be vulnerable and reveal yourself to one another, you allow the bond to become stronger and more intimate. You each are honored by receiving the truth from your man or woman. Truth and trust begin to weave a tight and unique connection. By becoming more emotionally "naked" about oneself with your partner, sex becomes more charged, more passionate. An exhilarating intimacy dimension is yours if you are willing to communicate with and trust in your partner.

TRUTH TELLING IS A CHALLENGE

Almost everyone has had the experience of assuming that one knows a partner only to be surprised or at times even shocked to find that one apparently does not. Most of us have also had the experience of thinking we know ourselves, only to be surprised at our own truth in a particular situation. We have been stronger than we believed we could be, angrier than we expected, or more hurt than we could justify. Truth has unending layers both for ourself and our partner. Just when we thought we had the man or woman figured out, he or she is liable to surprise us. Just when we have all our stories of our childhood making sense, we learn some new fact about our parents or siblings that changes our entire view of what makes us tick.

It's also true that many of us cannot be truthful at all times with our partner primarily because we have trouble being truthful with ourself. Yet we continue trying to shine the beacon of truth on the relationship because we believe that it enlivens and enriches the connection. We usually cannot tell the entire truth to our parents, our children, and certainly not our coworkers. We have truthful relationships with a few friends and hopefully with our partner. The truthful exchange then becomes a luxury, one we would not risk with others. It is an honor to give and receive, yet it is also demanding; because for the truth to continue to emerge, it must be accepted. When your partner tells you something important, it does no good if you respond with "You don't really mean that" or "I don't believe you" or "Don't say that." Instead, embrace his or her honesty and openness by saying, "Tell me more," "How does that feel?" and "What else?" In this way, you will validate the truth and open the connection even further.

When we play dodgeball with the truth, we become nimble and hard to catch. Like Peter Pan, we are delightful, childlike, perhaps even fascinating, but not real. Such men and women have energetic or fun sex, but if they are not in touch with their authentic self, then the intensity of their sexual connection will be limited. They have yet to mature into the deeper layers of exchange where the wonderful intricacies of our souls are revealed. Sex stays on the surface of the physical and doesn't dig deeper to the level of the emotional.

There is, however, an even more negative side to the intimacy dimension than simply not being in touch with your authentic self. When we find out something about ourself or our lover that is *deeply* disappointing, we experience betrayal. When the trust has been dishonored, the weaving is damaged. Such betrayal can come in many forms, but sexually speaking it is usually an affair. Short or long, once or many times, actual intercourse or emotional "intercourse," an affair with someone else can poison a relationship. Anyone who has struggled with the aftershocks of "affair earthquakes" knows how ungrounded the connection then feels. Everything is questioned: Do we rebuild? Do we separate and make lives elsewhere? Do we save or reclaim any aspects of the old relationship? Will there ever be safe ground again?

Lovers can learn how to enrich their intimacy dimension. This steadfast hope inspires countless women and men out of their sexual doldrums or anxious, hurt hearts.

SILENCE, THE POISONOUS TOAD

One of the primary challenges of the intimacy dimension is keeping the channels of communication open, but without true openness and exchange, a couple's sexual connection will begin to falter, and one or both of you will withdraw.

Jane and Sean were immediately drawn to each other when they met in Mexico. Jane was vacationing and Sean was there on business. They spent a few days casually interacting around the pool at the hotel, and by the end of the first week they had sex. Safe sex, Jane hastened to tell me. But she continued the story by saying that one night a few days later, Sean revealed to her the emotional detachment that he had practiced for much of his life and the trouble it had caused him. At the end of his previous relationship he had realized that he was guilty as charged, by several former girlfriends, of the habit of not revealing anything about his inner thoughts. After he admitted to himself that he had sabotaged his last relationship because he would not bridge the gap of intimacy, he finally understood, through individual counseling, that hiding his true self was a defense left over from his childhood when he would protect himself from the angry tirades and irrational behavior of his alcoholic parents. If nothing he said was accepted or "right" to his mom or dad, he just wouldn't say anything, folding away his personality and hiding it safely. This defense reaction affected all of his relationships with people. Specifically, it had destroyed his connection with a woman he had loved. She had revealed all, had honored him with her trust, and he had been like a clamshell, with all his emotions hidden.

For hours that night Sean and then Jane revealed aspects of themselves that they had never shared with a lover, certainly not a new lover, and in the wee hours of the morning, they made love in a new, more intense way. Sean vowed he would never hide from intimacy and revealing the truth again. Jane did not even have words for how powerful that lovemaking was, but she described how tears ran down her face with the intensity of the experience. She and Sean had opened a new, precious dimension of sex, one that continues for them today.

When couples withhold information about themselves and don't communicate with their partner at a deep, personal level, sex will not have depth and richness. Silence begins to reign in the relationship, affecting all the corners of its garden. Sexually, this silence deadens the passion and intensity, and sex becomes lifeless. Often what I call "sex by rote" becomes the standard.

This kind of silence between partners is common. We are not mute, of course, we just keep most details about ourself (how we feel, what we think, what we want, long for, or regret) to ourself. We may feel that when we try to tell the truth, to explain our opinion or view of the world, we get into an argument. One man I met described the feeling as "a why didn't you handle it this way" debate. He said that it was just easier to keep quiet. Ironically, he and his wife both believed that they still had a good connection, especially sexually. But they had an air of cautiousness about them. There was a hesitancy, a holding back, which I saw as a lack of the freedom of truth. This kind of silence is insidious. Like the poisonous toad who sits unblinking between the two of you, she watches everything and misses nothing. She won't often jump, but her presence is undeniable. And she does not enhance the bedroom!

Silence on the part of one partner while the other is trying to coax out the truth is also a common pattern. Often women find themselves keeping the conversation going. They tend to want more intimacy and seek out opportunities to discuss their feelings and thoughts. However, in my experience, women also often complain that they feel as if they're doing all the talking, all the sharing. Men sometimes play the innocent, defending themselves with "I just don't know what she wants to hear" statements. The silent one has the power of passive resistance. It is as if the relationship has taken on the aspect of a poker game: the player who is the most impassive comes out the winner. Probably true if you are playing poker, but definitely not if you are striving for multidimensional sex!

CURIOSITY CAN CARRY THE DAY

Boredom can kill the intimacy dimension almost as surely as betrayal; it is just a slower demise. Once we begin to know and love someone, then we begin to imagine how to delight him or her. We ask ourself, how can I excite this person whom I love? How can I make him or her happy? A palpable energy comes from engaging with the person we love. At the beginning of a relationship, this kind of communication feels effortless and happens spontaneously. However, with the passage of time and when the effects of familiarity take hold, many of us stop being inquisitive or forget to engage our partner at this level. We have decided that we know our partner, know the authentic self, the "truth," and we are so certain of this that we stop exploring our lover.

By reengaging in curiosity in the intimacy dimension, you can avoid boredom in your relationship. Obviously we can all feel bored at times, and it is difficult to always feel curious about the person we love. Similar to a kind of laziness, we grow so accustomed to what we already know (and assume) about our partner, we stop checking in with him or her. Deciding to look at your lover with "new eyes" once a week or to hear him or her with "new ears" can be quite amazing. And certainly, touching your lover's body as if you were exploring it for the first time awakens the sense of novelty.

We've spoken a lot about the power of communication, but another important facet of a healthy, thriving intimacy dimension is having wonderment and fun.

Why is the game of seduction so intoxicating? Energizing? Fun? Mystery, tension, and excitement build as we move toward the climax. This climax could be the final stripping off of clothes, the first kiss, or the thrill of penetration.

In the same way that sex is a mating game or ritual, it also is about play. And couples often come to me wanting to know certain techniques they can use at home or in their lives in general for creating or re-creating the spark of those first evenings together. The primary recommendation I make is to have them consciously adjust their attitude to one of curiosity, of intrigue.

When I met them, Melanie and Jake had moved several times in the preceding eight years. Melanie was exhausted and frustrated from being forced to adjust to each move required by Jake's career. It had been up to her and the children to reestablish the family in each new community, while Jake was focused on a new job.

Melanie remembered great sex when they married twelve years earlier, but that was before pregnancies, children, and of course Jake's careerism. She said that Jake had changed also, that the more he focused on his career, the more serious and sad he had become. Melanie was just about to give up. When I asked her how she was feeling now, she didn't hesitate to say "bored." She said without Jake's active involvement in the relationship, she had withdrawn sexually.

When I spoke with Jake, he complained mainly about the lack of a good sexual relationship. He could tell that Melanie was just "servicing him" at this point, and he wanted more for both of them.

Then we had a breakthrough.

Halfway through our consultation, Melanie shifted from defending her sexual withdrawal to make a poignant observation about what had happened to Jake. She said that what she missed the most, what she longed for, was the "playful Jake." She felt that his humor and joy of life had been stripped away.

Jake became quiet and visibly sad, because he knew it was true. He missed the old Jake as well.

Melanie and Jake decided that day to make sex their arena for excitement and nourishment. They agreed that each of them would take responsibility for initiating sex in a new and perhaps even wacky way every week. They sent each other "sexual invitations" and began teasing each other sexually. They were determined to start having fun again. When Melanie and Jake called several weeks later, they reported making love in a whole new way. Not only was their sexual exchange revitalized, but Melanie felt her angry silence melting away.

Melanie now felt much more honored sexually by Jake. His attention to her feelings and to consciously pleasuring her reconnected Melanie to what I call the goddess, that wonderful feminine energy that partakes of sensual power. And Jake was delighted. He had changed his work schedule so he could take walks with her in the morning, a routine she loved. He never wanted the stony silence to reign again in their relationship.

But then Jake faced a challenge from his career once again, with a new job in a city far enough away that he would need to go on Sunday evenings and return on Thursday afternoons. It was a temporary assignment, but they were appropriately concerned about the separation. I asked if Melanie could join Jake every other week on Wednesday in the city so they could have an evening alone as adults and then come home together on Thursday, and they eagerly responded by saying they could definitely arrange to do that. Melanie and Jake had creatively changed a difficult situation that would have caused emotional distance in the past into one that was likely to increase their intimacy.

Complicated issues sometimes require thoughtful, complicated solutions. But without open communication and the willingness to be honest, even if it is difficult for you or your partner, you will never even get the chance to repair what has been lost.

VOICE MAIL RELATIONSHIPS

Couples can also get stuck in another kind of communication gap. Instead of really telling their partner or lover what they are feeling, they verbalize only on the surface, where they think it is safer or just easier. Partners who have been together for a long time may get into the routine of just passing one another in the halls of their busy lives. They unconsciously forget to talk to one another and merely trade the necessary information: what time is dinner, who will pick up the kids, when is your mother coming to visit. They stop speaking about themselves as people. This kind of silence of the self, where couples stop sharing themselves with each other, further erodes their connection.

I call these voice mail relationships. Partners communicate the essentials of life via the handy, dandy machine. "Honey, remember to stop by the store to get a bottle of wine for the dinner at the Smiths'." "Darling, I have to be in San Francisco for meetings next week, they just set them up, sorry about our plans on Wednesday." Yes, we get a lot done, but where are the long conversations about where each one is going in life, about whether we are doing what we were put on the face of the earth to do, about what our partner means to us? These important exchanges get swept away in the business of day to day.

Mary and Mitch had met at the University of Chicago. They were intellectuals who said clearly that they valued honesty. In fact, one of the reasons they had married was that each was the first person who was able to be completely truthful with the other. They had risked a great deal of vulnerability with one another to achieve the reward of intimacy. When they came to see me, the toll of the kids, financial pressures, and life in general had worn them down. But worst of all, they felt distant from each other, almost unreachable. They no longer had time for long talks or casual intimacy. There were no more road trips with hours of sharing their deepest thoughts. They felt committed at the heart level and still had sex regularly, but their connection was lackluster. Making love felt like part of the household routine, and each of them told me it had "lost the spice."

When I asked them what they missed the most from their early days together, they replied almost simultaneously, "Our talks." For them, a lack of intimate exchange had snuffed out the spark. Each really wanted to know the truth about what the other was feeling and experiencing. Since that spark had been the basis for their sexual fire, it was no wonder that their connections had become infrequent and lackluster. Their sex had fed on the truth, on deep sharing of things no one else knew; it was the core of their sexual intimacy.

Another couple described how they had fun sex with a frequency that was above average compared to their friends'. They joked about sex, felt that they were free sexually, but there was one place they did not go sexually. They could not open the intimacy door. Most of their communication stayed superficial. Their observations about each other centered on such phrases as "Well, that is just how women are" or "You can't expect anything else from a man," as if the other were from an alien species. Not that we all don't occasionally joke about men and women as a group, but there was a bitter edge to these comments. They had given up speaking the truth to each other. They had lost the skill of intimate communication, and their sexual connection had suffered.

Countless women in sexuality workshops have complained about this lack of intimate life in their marriage, and often, many blame the kids. So much is going on with the sports, the homework, the teenage rebellion, and the electronic invasion of the home, that we barely make it through the day intact. For these women and their men, time away may be the only answer, even if just for a night. When you go out as a couple, the conversation should not be about the kids, even though they are important; it should be about you and your intimate life.

BICKERING AND THE BITE OF SARCASM

Another communication problem keeping us separate and distant from our partner is the habit of bickering or verbal antagonism. One couple who came to see me about the lack of sex in their marriage were quite confused as to what had happened to their once passionate relationship. Both were attorneys from the Southwest, and I noticed at once that they seemed superb at arguing. Pamela and Sid really could not agree on the time of day. Pam would say that it was a quarter past the hour and Sid would correct her, "No, it's really ten past." It was exhausting being in the room with their antagonistic energy.

Of course, neither took responsibility for their two-year celibacy. Their language was peppered with "you never," "you always," and "that is not what I said." Being right seemed much more important than being loved. And though both Sid and Pam declared that they wanted to be sexually intimate, neither was willing to give an inch. Stalemate.

They had developed this style out of a general irritability with their lives. Each was under tremendous pressure at work, and when they came home and began to ventilate about their cases, their colleagues, their clients, the other would offer "Well, you should have . . ." or "Why didn't you . . ." These reactions felt like salt in the wound for these two highly competitive people. Soon, they could not risk vulnerability even with each other, at least not verbally.

I taught them touch hands.

Touch hands is an adaptation of the tai chi game called push hands. In push hands, partners face each other, feet slightly apart, knees bent, and by pushing with the forearms and hands, try to throw their opponent off balance. In touch hands, partners touch fingertips while in a bent-knee stance for stability. A gentle forward and back rhythm of the partners' "centers" is established. Then one partner begins to move his or her hands about in creative ways, while the other follows, maintaining a light contact with the fingers. This kind of leading and following can magically break down the door of disconnection or stop the cycle of verbal debate and arguing through its quiet, focused simplicity.

Sid and Pamela could not talk when doing touch hands! They could not debate, correct, challenge, or defend. They had to learn to let the other lead and be the follower; each also took the lead and was followed. Then they had to practice having no leader so that they would pay attention to the subtle give-and-take between their fingertips. Here was intimacy without speech, and the result was amazing.

Pamela could not believe how much this exercise changed her feelings about her husband. She finally saw a side of him that was sensitive, attentive, and responsive to her. Sid finally relaxed his defenses enough to have a real exchange with his high-powered wife.

Touch hands is a powerful tool for breaking patterns of verbal debate, and it can be quite revealing of how a relationship can get stuck in a dynamic. During one workshop when touch hands was being practiced by the couples, I observed the exaggerated position of one of the pairs. The woman was bent backward with her husband leaning over her. She angrily broke the connection and burst out, "See! This is what you are always doing to me. You are always overpowering me."

The man looked shocked. "No," he responded, "I wasn't trying to overpower you. I just couldn't feel any pressure from your fingertips. I couldn't find you." It was a revealing moment about the dynamics of their relationship and provided a touchstone for further conversations about how they could begin to relate sexually without this misunderstanding.

CRAFTY CHAMELEONS

We may start a relationship with the full intention of being truthful and honest about who we are. But many of us unconsciously mask our true selves and become what I call chameleons. When people want so much for their partner to like them, they can become chameleonlike. Consciously or unconsciously, we find out what the other person wants and try to fit that image.

Women are especially prone to this kind of reinvention or masking of the self. In spite of all the lip service paid to equality between women and men, a lot of young girls are still raised to catch and please a man. They are taught that when they grow up, they will become someone's wife or mother, and to accomplish this goal, they will need to adapt to what men want. And though this is slowly changing and many women are basing their identities on their careers or other relationships, they are sometimes still afraid to explore, learn, and accept who they truly are sexually. In a relationship, these women then focus their energy on pleasing their partner and being the person they think he wants. For these chameleons, life becomes an act, a drama in which they constantly pretend. And sexually, the chameleon is limited to stiff, self-conscious sex.

Before my present marriage (which has happily lasted a quarter century), I was briefly married to another man whom I desperately wanted to make happy. I thought I knew how to do that: find out what he wanted and then become that. Simple! It was crazy of course and got me into a marriage that was a sham. I was an expert chameleon for a while, but it was exhausting and impossible to continue. He really did not know what he wanted anyway and ended up having an affair with an eighteen-year-old drug addict whose baby he had delivered in medical school.

The thing that struck me so forcefully at the time, besides my hurt, was that he could not have found anyone more different from me. I was taking premed courses in preparation for medical school. I thought I was doing my best to be what Jim wanted and needed in a partner, and it felt like a cosmic joke to recognize what was actually attractive to him.

For me it was a bitter lesson. But thankfully, I learned it early in my life, so that I had plenty of time to vow never to turn myself inside out in a futile attempt to be someone other than my authentic self. Sometimes, affairs have a way of waking us up. The splash of icy water stuns us at first, but later we can view the truth of the situation and the relationship from a much clearer vantage point.

Barbara also was a chameleon but in a different way. She had been a shy young girl and was still quiet. She married John right out of high school, and after twenty-four years of marriage she still loved him deeply. Her problem was that she spent much of her waking hours trying to become whatever anyone else wanted her to be. There was John, her mother-in-law, her own mother, the teachers at school, her minister, the neighbors; Barbara pleased everyone but herself. Finally, she admitted to me softly, she had had a nervous breakdown. She just couldn't do it anymore, and she collapsed into an unresponsive heap. Changing colors to match her environment did not work any longer. Feeling exhausted and depleted, Barbara just gave up.

Many of us have probably been close to where Barbara was stuck: our energy is gone; we have no sense of vitality and no sense of sexuality. We are so disconnected from our authentic self that we do not even know where to begin to find the truth. Barbara had done this work of finding her authentic self several years before I met her, and it had made her a woman capable of the truth and capable of an authentic relationship with her husband.

Barbara and John now take good care of the intimacy dimension. They schedule time for each other alone; they reveal their worries, thoughts, and feelings. As they put it, "We have to do this if we want to be healthy. It's not a choice."

THE SEVERING STING OF AN AFFAIR

In some cultures, affairs seem almost to be taken for granted, but in most committed relationships, affairs hurt, and the aftershocks create a domino effect: the secrecy of an affair destroys the relationship's trust, the threat of being replaced raises its ugly head, and one or both partners are caught in an endless search for "What does she have that I don't?" or "What did he do with you that I haven't?"

Jesse and Marilyn plopped down in my office chairs. With no preamble, Jesse announced that Marilyn had had an affair the previous year and they were still struggling with that. At forty-three, Jesse looked much younger. The previous year, he had taken over his family's business in Texas and consequently was now feeling financially secure. But he was anything but emotionally secure. When I asked him more about his feelings, he began to tell me how he still had to deal daily with his controlling mother, who had taken over leadership of the company after the death of his father when Jesse was a teenager. She had "given" him the company a few years ago, but not really. All major decisions could still be vetoed by her, and Jesse still had to dance his mother's dance. However, Marilyn's affair remained the primary source of his insecurity.

I asked Marilyn to explain her side of the story. What had happened? She began by speaking about all of the years that

Jesse had falsely accused her of having affairs. His constant accusations had made her feel as if he didn't trust her. Then finally, lonely and mistrusted, Marilyn had had the affair she had so long been accused of having. As is often the case, she discovered that being with another man was not what she wanted. She was sorry about the affair and said she really knew for the first time how much Jesse loved her because he was willing to give the marriage another chance. She even ventured a guess that she might have had the affair in part to see if Jesse cared.

This couple was in touch with their love for each other (connected in the heart dimension), but had to repair the container of trust between them (in the intimacy dimension). Jesse had habitually kept his own counsel, was a master of silence, and wore a look of sad forbearance. I asked him if, before the affair, he had ever shared the truth of how much he loved his wife with Marilyn; he said not really. I asked if he shared with his boys how much they meant to him, and he shook his head.

Here was a man so deeply afraid of revealing his vulnerability that he would actually create what he feared the most: no trust and no real connection with the human beings he loved so deeply. As Jesse began to look at his part in the drama of the past year, he also began to see that he could change the conditions that had contributed to the lack of intimacy. He began by telling Marilyn about his work daily, by scheduling one-on-one time with each of his boys and with his wife, and by using the "cut a deal" process with Marilyn to schedule sex that was not time-constrained, that gave them space for intimacy, which was crucial to the exchange of truth. These changes began to make Jesse feel more powerful and in control. Marilyn still felt ashamed of her behavior, but she had learned whom she really wanted to spend her life with and therefore had more hope than ever before of a vibrant, truthful, sexual marriage.

For some couples, affairs actually ignite the spirit of competition. For instance, I've seen many women begin to see their husband in a new light; her man suddenly becomes more sexually attractive and she avidly wants him back. Other couples will finally unlatch the door to a deeper truth and feel "What more is there to lose?"

Still other couples will acknowledge that the affair is a symptom of what they have both long known, that their relationship has been lacking the heart connection, and that the affair occurred is further proof of the emotional distance between them. In this case the affair is just the final act in a play whose many scenes have been building to its inevitable conclusion.

Unfortunately, many of us have had to deal with affairs, either our own or our partner's. An affair makes us face challenges. In my case, my ex-husband's affair first made me confront the reality that I had nothing more to lose. I realized then how utterly different he and I were, down to the roots of our beings. The crack in the container of trust let in the light and exposed such a basic divergence that we could never patch it over.

Can a marriage survive an affair? Yes. Can it survive whole and vibrant? I believe it can. Couples have come in to see me ten and fifteen years after an affair with a philosophical perspective on the past, explaining that in the end, the affair caused them to go to a deeper level with each other. It was as if they had seen all the skeletons in Bluebeard's cellar and could now clean out the lies and mistrust and begin again with truth as the foundation.

But I also believe that affairs require couples to seek professional help. The issues arising out of an affair are almost impossible to heal without the perspective of a third, hopefully wise, being. I have seen many couples try to sweep the entire episode under the rug. The affair may remain hidden, never talked about, but each partner always knows that it is there and often stumbles on the mess while trying to go on with life.

As a counselor I have facilitated the healing of many couples' intimacy dimension by providing a safe place and the encouragement to share truths. Sometimes the hurt and betrayal are so severe that a couple is cut off from each other completely, eroding the basis of their relationship. This kind of erosion needs profound healing for the couple to get realigned in this dimension.

Elaine and Mike were such a couple. They lived in Malibu and had struggled hard to make their food franchise a tremendous success. They were both headstrong and volatile. They were also very verbal and believed that they had always been truthful with each other. But they also admitted not trusting each other either.

When Mike had found out about Elaine's affair with the neighborhood Porsche dealer, he had exploded. He plotted revenge and even considered putting out a contract on the guy. And believe me, Mike was capable of doing it! However, they had been high school sweethearts, and something about this long connection made them want to seek counseling, even though they both agreed that their marriage was over.

Looking at the seven dimensions as they applied to their sexual relationship, Elaine and Mike saw that the main defect was in intimacy. Vulnerability was hidden at all costs, and they both lived by the rule that the only one you trust is yourself. When I told them the story of the Zen warrior, the man so proud and consumed with revenge that he would not pull the arrow out of his chest, Mike immediately knew that he was letting this wound fester. He realized that he had to pull the arrow of bitterness out if he was ever going to heal, but he had a hard time imagining doing it. Elaine said she had a whole war chest of injuries done to her over the years by Mike. She had not shared her authentic self for such a long time because she felt that they were adversaries. In gaining insight into why she had had the affair, she said she was a pushover for someone who would listen, who loved her even when she exposed her weaknesses.

Without intimacy, there is no basis for trust. Without trust, sex is tenuous. Without the truth, we are strangers. A vital intimacy dimension provides all the power and energy to bring your sexual relationship to a deeper, more meaningful level. The key is to commit to sharing the truth—about your lives, yourselves, and the world around you.

TECHNIQUES TO ENERGIZE
THE INTIMACY DIMENSION

In this dimension, first take stock and look honestly at your ability to be truthful, then ask your partner to do the same. If your other dimensions are in place (and you still love one another and are committed to your relationship), then you need to consciously and continuously foster this truth channel, allowing yourselves to be authentic no matter the past or fears of the future. *Remember, this is the person you want your mate to love.* Promise to begin again communicating from this place. This deep, powerful intimacy cannot happen without two vital ingredients: real sharing and trust. When both of you have spoken the truth about yourselves, and this truth is recognized and accepted, then true, enriching intimacy will flow, honoring your love and charging your connection with sexual vitality. So, expel the poisonous toad of silence, unhook the voice mail relationship, ban sarcasm, and refuse to be a love chameleon. The attitude of exploration and curiosity will bring back fun and hold boredom at bay. Take these techniques of the intimacy dimension as suggestions and devise your own game plan. One of you is probably more comfortable with this dimension, so let this person lead, but be sure they are thanked, and not resisted, for their efforts.

1. TOUCH HANDS

Play this game each day for one week as a way to connect nonverbally and intimately, just to "feel" where the other person is. Remember in push hands partners face each other, feet slightly apart, knees slightly bent, and by pushing with the forearms and hands, try to throw their opponent off balance. In touch hands, partners touch fingertips while in a bent-knee stance for stability. First the gentle forward-and-back rhythm of the partners' pelvic "centers" is established; then one partner begins to move his or her hands about in creative ways—faster, slower, or with large or small movements—while the other follows, maintaining a light contact at the fingers. Doing this exercise brings new perceptions to the kinesthetic dynamic (remember this is one of our sensual inputs) and allows communication without talk.

The touch hands exercise also helps you to open up sensual channels, creating energy that flows between you. The parallel to the constant give-and-take of a loving sexual interaction is clear, along with the need to remain open and sensitive to subtle changes in energy and intention felt in those sensitive fingertips.

2. TRUTH WEEK

Emphasize intimacy for one week, and schedule ten minutes a day for first one and then the other to speak, unin-

terrupted, about what is important in life. Resist the temptation to comment on your lover's observations even if it
is to agree with them. Being listened to completely is a
powerful experience, as you will find when it is your turn
to speak. And listening without responding sharpens your
focus. Pretend you are interviewing an important person
and you want to hear every syllable he or she utters!

3. LET-IT-GO EXERCISE

Consider the radical act of releasing all the residue from
any betrayals, emotional or physical, that exist between
you. When you discover resentment, old stuff, honestly ask
yourself if you are nursing it and whether you are ready to
let it go. Try acting for a short while as if it were gone and
see how intimate you feel. If you cannot close the emotional gap with your partner, do not stay stuck. Get some
short- or long-term help from a professional counselor to
clear away the debris.

4. CURIOSITY CHALLENGE

Practice curiosity toward your partner. Every week for a
month, find out one new thing or something that has
changed about him or her. You may think that there is
nothing different, but we all know inside that we are
always changing, adjusting, discovering parts of ourself.
Trust me, that is going on with your lover as well.

5. LOVE SPEAK

Talk when you make love. Share an erotic fantasy, memory, or something sexual you have noticed about your
partner. Describe what your lover is doing to you, how you

are feeling, what you are noticing in your body—the swelling, wetness, fullness—and synchronize your erotic experiences to amp up the electricity between you.

6. SEXY STORIES

As I recommended in the desire dimension, reading a sexy story to each other, perhaps half in jest with foreign accents and half seriously, can create a fun, intimate atmosphere. The erotic world is waiting out there, and you can engage whatever part of it seems appropriate to you and your lover. Make sure that you have your intimacy radar turned on so that the two of you are enjoying the experience together.

7. HUMOR FEST

Delight your partner with funny stories, dirty jokes, the comics and cartoons. There is nothing better than a good laugh, and there are things that only the two of you can laugh about. Create a rich tapestry of special, intimate threads between you that is always being elaborated with humorous observations. It will stand you in good stead when not so funny things have to be faced.

KEEPING YOUR GARDEN FERTILE

Enriching the intimacy dimension takes practice and attention. First, both of you have to believe that offering the truth to each other is an honor and that taking the risk of being vulnerable is a big part of what makes us special to each other. Finding out what is going on with your lover is a continuous process. As in caring for a garden, the soil needs nutrients as much in fall and winter as it does in spring and summer. And unless these are replenished, the earth becomes depleted of the necessary elements for growth. We also change. What we are today, what we are capable of today, is different from two, five, or ten years ago. If you can learn to accept and indeed enjoy change in your mate, the garden continually bestows new and wondrous produce.

Relationships are also tender. I believe that couples not only have to create the soil of trust, they have to be vigilant about the weeds, the pests, the general condition of their garden. Are there stalks that need staking? Have weeds hidden the vibrant colors? Is there disease from mistrust that needs treating?

When we see our intimacy as precious, we will take care of it as well as we do any prized possession. The closeness and vulnerability of this dimension takes sex to a deeper level. It can take our breath away when we reveal something to our lover that even we are not proud of and they respond, "Yes, I know that about you, and I still love you." The self-acceptance is like a warm, gentle rain on the garden of the two of you; many beautiful things will emerge. We must remain open and ready for greater and greater degrees of truth. And remember, the truth really will set you free.

7

Creating a Pathway to the Soul

THE AWE OF THE AESTHETIC DIMENSION

Every truth is fragile, every knowledge must be learned over and over again, every night, that we grow not in a straight line but in ascending and descending and tilting circles and that what gives us power one year robs us of power the next, for nothing is settled, ever, for anyone. What makes this bearable is awe.

—CARLOS CASTANEDA

WHAT IS SEXUAL RADIANCE?

Have you ever felt yourself thrill at the sight of the sunset, as the great orange orb slid into a vast blue sea? Did you ever watch in awe as your newborn infant smiled for the first time, her face beaming with love? Remember lying in the grass on a June day, letting the sun warm your body as you watched the minute insect world, mesmerized by the complexity of nature? Have you ever looked at a piece of art—a sculpture, a painting—and felt transported by the starkness of its beauty?

This same transformative power that we have all experienced in art or nature can also be found, and exchanged, with your lover. When we see the essence of our lover, for however long or short, this ordinary being seems suddenly special, infused with grace and radiance. When this happens, we are awed. We are awed not by the details of how our man or woman looks, not by the accomplishments or the intelligence, but we are overwhelmed by the inner beauty, the radiance, the soul. When this radiance shines forth unencumbered, the sexual connection between two people begins to transcend age and circumstance and enters a place of pure beauty. However, to enter this exquisite chamber you need to believe that you are beautiful and that sex—the act itself—is an expression and embrace of this shared beauty.

The aesthetic dimension brings us face-to-face with the task of accepting how beautiful, how radiant, we are. In many cultures, including our own, this part of us, this inner beauty (what I am referring to as "essence") is called the soul. And even though the soul is abstract and intangible, we believe in its existence, without any objective proof, which is why, when we see or feel the soul of another person, we experience him or her as radiant.

I believe, to quote the author and thinker Thomas Moore, that the soul is the "seat of a relationship." Because of its constancy, the soul is the glue that keeps our relationship alive throughout the years. The soul of our relationship is that which supports us throughout the wear and tear on our bodies, during the trying years of raising children, and while we struggle to make ends meet and endeavor to achieve our goals.

But the soul is also what moves us from having adequate, ordinary sex to magnificent sex. The aesthetic dimension is the first stepping-stone into sex as a spiritual experience. Here we get in touch with our souls individually, and then the soul of the relationship, so that we are then able to reach beyond the earthly boundaries and experience sex at a higher level.

So many of the cultural messages we receive about sex indicate the best sex is when we are young, but in my experience, those couples who have exceptional sex are often older and have been together a long time. Their comfort with each other, their acceptance of their bodies, and their openness to each other's soul allows them the freedom and courage to reach beyond the ordinary to make sex a spiritual experience. The good news is that we do not have to wait for a particular age before we can have ecstatic sex. But we do have to uncover those factors that make us feel disconnected from our souls, which is why this dimension has the power to bring us face-to-face with our deepest fears about ourselves, those images that keep us from truly loving ourselves for who we are.

This dimension builds upon the ideas covered in the intimacy dimension, because in order to see the beauty—both inner and outer—of our lover and ourself, we also need to be communicating authentically, sharing real and significant aspects of who we are. To feel comfortable sharing and revealing ourselves, we need to feel safe. When one or the other partner is critical or judgmental, openness shrivels. Therefore, the challenge of the aesthetic dimension is to look beyond the imperfect bodies, the tired face, the worried expression, and to see our lover's essence in sharp, wondrous relief. When we do, we get in touch once again with the person with whom we fell in love—whether that was twenty, ten, or two years ago. When they notice us really seeing them, their radiance and inner beauty shines forth. This radiance is embodied by our individual sexual god or goddess.

THE SEXUAL GODDESS AND GOD WITHIN

Imagining yourself as a sexual god or goddess may seem outrageous, impossible, or just downright funny; however, the divine

qualities of mythic men and women are exactly what I am talking about in this dimension. If you allow yourself these qualities
of heroes and heroines, you can be larger-than-life, more grand,
more powerful, more irresistible, and fabulously sexual and
desirable.

A goddess revels in her femininity and connection to all
her sisters, to all of womankind. She believes in her compas-
sionate, sensual power and she uses her sexual force to both heal
and ignite her partner. She may be wanton, regal, joyful—any
of a number of moods—but she is deeply aware of her inner
radiance. Her connection to the deep feminine is unassailable
and gives her roots in a profoundly beautiful female sexuality.
Recognition and belief in the goddess can be claimed by any
woman, and it is glorious to observe.

Of course, men can and should connect with the essence of
a sexual god. This is not a god who is imperious or judgmental,
but one who is self-assured, vital, and virile. This man wel-
comes the goddess energy and is strengthened by it; he is open
to change but knows his own soul; he has the courage to recognize and reveal his radiance. When a man claims this part of
himself, his sexual power in the spiritual realm, he can ignite his
woman sexually and honors his and her divine nature.

If the soul of either individual is ignored, and someone's
radiance goes unacknowledged, a relationship may continue to
exist—the sex may feel satisfactory—but something is missing.

A sexual relationship in which two people are in touch
with their god and goddess aspects and see the inner radiance of
the other possesses these components:

1. Your partner is beautiful to you. Each of you is a god or
    goddess, especially during lovemaking.
2. You and your lover cherish each other, consciously rein-
    forcing the inner beauty of each other.

3. You feel unencumbered and free during sex.
4. You feel that you and your lover are soul mates.
5. You avoid criticism and judgment in your relationship.
6. You support each other's sexual-goddess and godlike qualities.

Before encountering the aesthetic dimension as clearly as I know it now, I always thought that my husband, David, and I had a great sexual relationship. We had sex about three times a week, which was satisfying to both of us. He was orgasmic, I was orgasmic. We could feel our love for each other, and often after sex, we would agree, "We needed that." What was not to like?

But underneath this surface satisfaction, I would sometimes hear a faint whisper: *Is this all there is?* If I were really honest with myself, I would have had to admit that our sex life was pretty ordinary, sometimes even boring. After all, it was the same bed in the same room in the same positions with the same guy.

I knew David and I were not alone in feeling this way, and I knew we needed to do something. But what? What would lift our sexual connection out of the realm of the ordinary and make it feel extraordinary? How could we reliably enter the realm of awesome sex?

Looking back on those feelings now, I see that we had not included, at least consciously, our souls during sex. In chapter 9 I will give you the details of our story, but the essential discovery was that the soulful connection can be created just as reliably as the sensual or heart connection. It does not have to descend upon us as a gossamer blessing without rhyme or reason; it can be invited and encouraged to be a beautiful fabric surrounding the relationship.

From my experience with David and in listening to the hundreds of men and women who have stepped through my office door in the last twenty years, I have come to describe this "missing" sexual element as the absence of a connection to the soul. For so many couples, life, sex, the relationship in general, aren't bad, yet are mundane. Absent are the moments of specialness, when making love felt as if you were charting the heavens and seeing into each other's spirit.

The reasons obscuring your or your partner's radiance and the causes that block you from accepting your god or goddess within are as varied as the individual personalities of the world. But there are some common themes. Some of us have never, ever felt radiant. We have been trained to look for what is wrong with us rather than what is right or beautiful. Sometimes we get caught up in the shame of a poor body image, hearing a recording in our head that says, "I'm too fat, too old, too clumsy." Or we get so caught up in the stress of our everyday lives that we become detached from that inner part of us where the soul lives and become blind to our own radiance or that of our partner. And finally, even if we were once "out there" as a glorious sexual being, we can bury our radiance in reaction to our partner. In our anger over criticism or in recoil from some judgment, we may hide our soul from our loved one in a vain attempt to protect our fragile ego.

SEX IS BEAUTIFUL

No matter how you were raised or which ethnic group you were born into, a common underlying belief in most cultures is that sex is depraved, a temptation, the road to ruin. I recently saw the strength of this association. For our twenty-fifth anniversary, David and I took a fabulous trip to France and Italy. While in the town of San Gimignano, in the Tuscany region of Italy, we went into a wonderful cathedral with extraordinary frescoes. On one wall were scenes from the Old Testament, on the opposite wall were scenes from the New Testament, and at one end were pictured the seven deadly sins falling downward in a spiral form. Lust, or desire, was at the bottom of the spiral, poised to enter hell.

Lust was also depicted as female (of course!), and in the painting, she was having her hair pulled out by one devil, while another devil poured boiling oil on her body, and a third she-devil was shoving a lance into her vagina! Considering these frescoes were pictorial moral lessons before people could read, what an image they were of what happens to the poor soul who gives in to sexual desire! There are many other historical warnings of the link between women's sexual desire and evil, such as images of the forbidden apple of carnal wisdom, and the sensual snake in Genesis, forcing both man and woman to be thrown out of the Garden of Eden. Samson lost his legendary strength when Delilah got ahold of his hair. And when John the Baptist rejected the sexual temptress Salome, she had his head brought to her on a platter!

The Judeo-Christian tradition is not the only religious tradition that views female sexuality as dangerous and powerful. In much of the Middle East and Asia, we have present-day shrouding of women. In Africa, ritualized female circumcision to deter pleasure from the sexual act is practiced on young women daily. In certain Islamic countries, feudalistic punishments of couples who find themselves in love outside the designated parameters are common. At the opposite extreme in the West, we have prominent members of religious movements giving in to the "temptations of sex," and we have esteemed members of both political parties brought low by sexual escapades that seem to be without a heart and soul connection.

When one or both partners have been raised in an environment where rigid or negative views of sexuality are taught, letting go of the negative and embracing the positive can be difficult. Rebecca and Les had struggled with messages that were not pathologic but that had inhibited both of them sexually. Many years ago Les had met and married Rebecca after returning from a stay in Israel, where he'd made an intensive study of the Torah. At that point Les viewed sex as suspect, and he had many restrictions about oral sex, intercourse, sensuality. Rebecca felt her sexual self retracting from him. She felt almost as if she contained something perverted within her feminine sexual self that Les judged as wicked or at least a temptation to stray from the path of good.

Their physical and emotional distance worsened when they were faced with a baby who had birth defects, requiring tremendous time and attention in its first year of life. Rebecca definitely did not feel radiant, and even if she did, she was not going to risk showing that to Les.

I do not know how Les's beliefs about sex altered over time; perhaps as his more zealous days as a young man were tempered by the love of his woman, he began to change. Whatever the reason, he now saw how his original attitude toward Rebecca's sexuality had soured their relationship. In my office, he said that his viewpoint had matured and he was now able to tell Rebecca that he thought she actually had the healthier approach to sex. He wanted to bathe in her sensuality and radiance, but he had a lot of repair work to do to make her believe that it was safe to reveal this aspect of herself to him.

Nancy and Alan faced a similar problem, although in this instance Nancy had taken to heart her Catholic parents' view of sexuality. They did not ever talk to her directly about sex, but the rules around dating and any contact with boys were strict.

There were good girls and there were bad girls, you were one or the other, pure or polluted, Madonna or whore. Nancy would never allow Alan to stimulate her genitally either manually or orally; she never of course did that to him.

As the years had passed, continually being around each other's body so much had led them to be more relaxed. Their participation in the couples workshop made them look at the beauty in the other through the lens of sexuality, and they actually began to see sex as an opportunity for expressing their deep commitment. Ultimately, they told me they were moved to tears during one lovemaking session when passion and beauty finally merged. Both Nancy and Alan were awed by the exquisite experience of deep sexual loving without any forbidden zones.

When couples or individuals get so completely isolated from their own or their partner's radiance, they will avoid soul sex at all costs. In this state, a sexual encounter has virtually no chance of unearthing the radiance of either partner. Indeed, such a negative view of sexuality is antithetical to radiance.

For all lovers, this dimension asks you, just as earlier ones did, to examine your associations and concepts surrounding sex. As we saw in the lust dimension, negative beliefs or associations with sex can lead to inhibition, shutting down your ability to feel desire. But in the aesthetic dimension, these restrictive beliefs can affect you at an even deeper level, cutting off your relationship with your sexual soul. Nancy and Alan were able to experience tremendous healing once they exposed the old, inaccurate views of sex that were getting in their way. However, in other cases I've seen, negative associations with sex require deeper analysis to understand and then to resolve. Here professional counseling may be helpful to women and men who can't seem able to detour around such crippling ideas. However, all of us can benefit by meditating on the profound gift that soul sex can bring. By keeping our focus on the ultimate prize, we hopefully feel motivation to let go of old beliefs.

LET GO OF YOUR BODY

When I speak about discovering the sexual goddess within, I am reminded of a passage from Clarissa Pinkola Estes, in her popular book *Women Who Run with the Wolves*:

> The body is like an earth. It is a land unto itself. It is as vulnerable to overbuilding, being carved into parcels, cut off, overmined, and shorn of its power as any landscape. . . . The hips, they are wide for a reason, inside them is a satiny ivory cradle for new life. A woman's hips are outriggers for the body above and below; they are portals, they are a lush cushion, the handholds for love, a place for children to hide behind. The legs, they are meant to take us, sometimes to propel us; they are the pulleys that help us lift, they are the anillo, the ring for encircling a lover. They cannot be too this or too that. They are what they are.
>
> There is no "supposed to be" in bodies. The question is not size or shape or years of age, or even having two of everything, for some do not. But the wild issue is, does this body feel, does it have right connection to pleasure, to heart, to soul, to the wild? Does it have happiness, joy? Can it in its own way move, dance, jiggle, sway, thrust? Nothing else matters.

This beautiful view of the body is what we need to release the fullness of our sexuality, yet how mercilessly critical we are. There are always laughs of recognition when I describe that inevitable day when women decide that they can no longer be "on top" during sex because then we would have to hold the skin of our face back with both our hands! We can only be on the bottom, where also our stomachs are flat and we look "good." This is more often a female problem; men can cruise around with a fairly big potbelly, and although they think they should lose a little weight, they don't think this should keep them from good sex. Habitually, we women allow cellulite, wrinkles, and the effects of gravity to shroud our sexual souls from our lovers. Fearful of exposure to criticism, women stay hidden aesthetically from themselves and their partners.

When women and men become distracted by the flaws they see in their bodies, they are unable to feel or believe in their own radiance. They are blind to their inner beauty, or soul, as they become caught up in their self-consciousness. Emma and Ralph came to see me because they felt enormously frustrated with the wall they seemed to have hit in their sex life. They described how loving their relationship had always been, and that they still, after fifteen years of marriage, felt deeply in love and bonded. I could see the love between them; it was tangible in the way they touched and looked at each other. But something wasn't working.

Ralph felt as if Emma had withdrawn, that a part of her was missing. When I asked Emma if she felt this was true, she nodded in agreement. Then she began to talk about how she had put on weight. She now felt so ashamed of being overweight that she no longer let Ralph touch or see her naked body. She dressed in the closet and never, ever wanted any lights on when they had sex.

Ralph confirmed that he understood she had become self-conscious about her body, but he wanted to know how he could make positive suggestions to Emma, letting her know that he loved her no matter what. He wanted to encourage her to become more physically healthy, but he was afraid of hurting her or making her feel defensive.

I asked him if he was sexually attracted to Emma and he said, "Yes!"

"Do you believe him?" I asked Emma. She gave us a reluctant look. It was clear she did not.

Then Ralph began to describe a beautiful statue of a Mayan woman they had seen in their travels to Mexico. The female statue depicted a large, round woman. Ralph said that the statue was beautiful, and that the woman's face reminded him of Emma's. Emma was deeply moved by Ralph's story and his clear attempt to make her feel better about her body.

This one incident may not have squelched Emma's bad feelings about herself, but she did admit that Ralph's willingness to be more vocal about how he loved her body helped. After several sessions in which we reviewed the seven dimensions of their relationship, Emma began to feel more comfortable with her body and her sexuality as well. As her self-acceptance increased, Emma felt herself become even more beautiful and radiant—to herself and to Ralph.

In fact, women who are well loved and allow that love to penetrate their inner being glow visibly because they feel the sexual goddess within. They are secure in their attractiveness to their mate, they like the way their body moves, dances, jiggles. The sensual language that is spoken between this woman and her lover translates into a palpable expansion of self, like a beautiful flower always blooming.

"Who am I kidding, trying to be a sexual goddess?" Diane said sarcastically. She had been married to Jerry for twenty-seven years and had worked out many of the negative sexual messages she had received growing up in a household dominated by an alcoholic, abusive father. Yet, years later, whenever her husband would get angry, Diane would recoil, even when Jerry's anger had nothing to do with her. But even her "jumpiness," as she put it, about that issue had lessened through the years. However, Diane got an A in self-criticism; she did not like her body, and she couldn't believe that Jerry did. She was unable to experience herself as sexually radiant, even though Jerry was absolutely eloquent in my office describing how he loved making love to her because of how beautiful she is.

Perhaps it was the early years of being torn down emotionally by her father, perhaps it was the codependence of her mother, whom Diane described as a "saint" to have put up with her father. Perhaps still it was the exhaustion that comes from being hypervigilant to others' feelings of anger. Whatever the exact cause, Diane found it hard to claim her sexual goddess.

As Diane was describing details of the emotional abuse in her past, tears ran down her cheeks. Jerry gently reached over and dried them with a Kleenex. Softly, he reminded her that at certain times she *had* revealed this goddess energy when they had made love. He remembered it vividly on several occasions and wanted her and them to experience this more often. Diane looked directly at him at that moment and gave him one of the most radiant smiles I have ever seen. Jerry was right, she had it, this beautiful energy, but she needed to believe that she deserved to own and share it.

Diane is not alone in feeling inadequate because she does not fit the cultural ideal of beauty. In the lust dimension we acknowledged the power of the media to affect our self-image and our self-esteem where impossible ideals make women and men feel inadequate to play the "mating game." Here in the aesthetic dimension, inadequacy has a subtler, in some ways more damaging effect, because it closes the door to sexual radiance, that ineffable quality that has the power to transform.

It is high time that we value these wonderful bodies of ours and that we believe in the power of the inner radiance, that we use them to make glorious love to the one we have chosen. For who else should see our joy?

STUCK ON THE OUTSIDE

Another way you can be prevented from releasing the god or goddess within is when you become habitually self-conscious, literally thinking from outside of the self instead of acting or feeling from within. Women and men can get stuck on developing and maintaining their exterior, ignoring their interior, where the soul lives. Men often state in workshops that they "really want her to let go." That this "turns them on." However, when a woman is intensely externally directed, focused primarily on her hair, facial expressions, genital appearance, she is almost outside herself. It is as if she has taken to observing herself instead of being connected with her deep abiding self. Looking down at herself from the bedroom ceiling, she is now two: the woman watching and the woman having sex, and her man is holding only half of his woman.

Like Diane above, Jane also withheld herself from her partner, Tim, but in a different way, for different reasons. Jane was a thirty-four-year-old former model. She was extraordinarily attractive. Tall and lean, with a mass of chestnut hair, she came close to the media's image of an ideal. She and Tim had been together for five years and married two. They came to see me when Tim began complaining that Jane felt disinterested or detached when they made love. After getting to know them and listening to them, I concluded that it was Jane's awareness of her own beauty that was stifling her. She was trained to watch her pose, her expression, her body, from outside herself. It made her a great model. She had also become so used to people finding her attractive, to heads turning when she walked into a room, that it was as if she believed that was all people saw in her. In fact, her striking beauty isolated her, and over time she developed an inner loneliness. Sexually, this belief kept her withdrawn and distant even with Tim. Spiritually she stayed on the surface, self-conscious, aware of her external beauty but unable to connect with her inner radiance.

Once Tim convinced her that it was what lay underneath her outer beauty that made him truly love her, Jane was able to begin slowly letting go of the constant awareness of her appearance while beginning to reveal her inner beauty.

Remember, sharing of our authentic selves means allowing ourselves to be vulnerable. If we hear an internal voice saying we are too fat, too ugly, too old, or even too beautiful as in Jane's case, we are not going to be in a place that encourages revealing ourselves. Lovers who lose sight of their inner radiance become blinded and are unable to see past the surface. At the same time, if we hear the voice of another criticizing any aspect of our person, we will also shut down. Either way, our radiance is blocked.

CRITICISM CUTS

Our sexual skin is thin. We hate to be criticized, and most of us will go to great lengths to avoid the sting of cutting remarks. We take the slightest turn of the head, the hesitation in a caress, the "constructive" comment, as if we were being condemned. A lover's judgment can feel harsher than any criticism we've ever received. Radiance and its beauty have little chance to surface in a relationship tarnished by frequent criticism.

Eric was articulate in expressing his love for Simone as they sat together in my office. Their three-year relationship was truthful and deeply caring. Eric saw Simone as sensual and erotic, yet he could not explain why at times he did not feel like making love. Prior to the night before their consultation with me, it had been six weeks since they had had sex. As Eric described his sexual history, he told of an important teenage love that had ended when he was twenty. During this high school romance, his mother had died; at the time he was only seventeen. Two crucial losses for a young man.

Later Eric had actually tried unsuccessfully to resume his relationship with his first lover. Discouraged, he had then had many sexual relationships without much emotional content. Finally he'd met Simone. During that first consultation, I soon noticed that Eric also had the "habit" of judgment and was quite critical of himself and even of Simone at times. Nothing was ever quite right for Eric. Everything could be better, and most people and experiences just didn't measure up to what he thought they should. Why, you ask, do people like Eric have this habit? It protects them from disappointment. When things, situations, relationships, don't work out, they can always say that they really expected the negative or disappointing outcome. Radiance, shmadiance, Eric didn't want to go there.

Simone had experienced the aesthetic dimension before and wanted to have that connection with Eric. When I asked them to look in each other's eyes in the office during the soul-gazing exercise, Eric had trouble.

At that moment he realized he was afraid to let Simone in. He was apprehensive about not only seeing her radiance, but even more about revealing his own. A sense of unworthiness made him cautious, something that I believe began many years before with those two traumatic losses of his mother and his first love.

Jeff and Mary were no strangers to counseling. They had taken on several issues during their long-term relationship and had resolved them successfully. Now they were coming in to address sexuality concerns that were still not resolved. Specifically, Mary felt that Jeff's controlling personality made her unable to fully let go. During sex—whether they were in a soft and loving mood or one that was more lusty and passionate—Mary wanted more of the loving touch to make her relax and feel open.

Jeff responded by turning to Mary and, taking her hands in his, telling her, "I want the kind of relationship where you can look at me and be loving and where I can love you in return."

Mary smiled back at him, and then, unexpectedly for the soft moment that seemed to be occurring between them, Jeff said, "See, you are smiling that smile again. I want you to remove that smile from your face and be serious about this."

Mary physically recoiled, saying, "I don't want to stop smiling."

But she did, of course. It was a perfect example of how Jeff is habitually judgmental toward her, deflating her being with his need to control even when and how she smiles. He admitted that his gratuitous comment had certainly changed the atmosphere in the room, but he staunchly defended his freedom to make the observations he thought were true at the time. Of course, that was his right, but he had better be ready for the emotional and spiritual downfall from these "observations" and directives. After we explored this pattern a bit more, Jeff thought that the habits of judgment and control had developed early in life. When I asked Jeff why, he explained that he had an influential older brother who had always been harsh with him.

Usually individuals learn this behavior from having experienced it themselves. As we began to dig deeper, it became clear to me that Jeff criticized Mary to deflect intimacy. It was actually because he believed he was not worthy of Mary's love. Yet his constant or habitual self-criticism was internalized to such a degree that he only felt more vulnerable and unworthy, thereby hiding his soul even more. His criticism of his wife helped him to maintain control, by keeping her "off base." The result was that she could not win, whether she was open or not.

In reality, Jeff actually revered his wife and thought that she was a wonderful human being. His challenge was to first get in touch with his love for her, and then to get in touch with his own soul, letting himself give up the control (i.e., judgment) of himself and her. Mary knew this about Jeff at some level, having sensed his vulnerability, but often she could not get by his lacerating comments.

I counseled this couple by suggesting they develop a contract in which they both began to initiate some type of sensual and loving contact—each and every day—that did not necessarily lead to intercourse. Jeff had to recognize his sharp tongue and prevent himself from criticizing Mary.

Untangling the roots of judgment and criticism can often feel like stumbling through a maze. The task requires work and persistence. The reward, however, is often profound: the uncovering of a soul—yours or your partner's—can bring magnificent light into your relationship.

Some of us who have lost a parent or an important person in our life find connection at the soul level to be frightening, as if when we get close to another human, we risk loss and terrible hurt. We become critical as a defense against future hurt, and it works well because when we are judgmental, deep soulful connection evaporates. That defense may not have been the only reason for Jeff's reluctance to encounter the beauty and radiance of Mary, but with this understanding, he could begin to work with his hesitation as a first step to a deeper, more soulful connection to the woman he loved.

THE VIGILANT LOVER

The vigilant lover is on the constant lookout for censure or judgment—even though the present relationship may be free of criticism. Perhaps the lover experienced a lot of judgment as a child or in a previous relationship. Regardless of how loving and healthy her present relationship is, she stands on guard, waiting for the sting of an arrow. This static pose, however, prevents her from revealing her radiance.

Sexually, the vigilant lover is afraid to let her guard down. She is self-conscious and fearful of being hurt, so she keeps her inner radiance well hidden. Sam and Karen, a couple in our sexuality workshop, had grown emotionally distant. They described having had a wonderful passionate courtship many years before, but a hard first year of marriage had laid the stones of subsequent difficulty. Specifically, Sam's mother had lived in their house during the first year of their marriage. Not only was this intrusive in their day-to-day life, it was impossible to have any sexual privacy. Karen described lying in bed able to hear her mother-in-law turn the pages of her newspaper—that's how thin the walls were! Karen felt judged by the mere presence of her mother-in-law, but Sam exacerbated the situation by being unable to establish any boundaries to block his mother's judgmental comments.

Years later, Karen was still hearing the negative voices in her head, and she knew that she was holding back a crucial, important part of herself from their sexual relationship. When they came to see me, both were intent on understanding and getting in touch with this "missing piece" of Karen's.

As we went through the dimensions, we struck upon a nerve: Karen still felt uncomfortable during sex, as if someone were watching. When she was able to trace this feeling back to the days when her mother-in-law lived with them, she suddenly saw how deeply affected she'd been. At the same time, Sam saw that his putting up with his mother and not being more attuned to the nourishment of their sexuality had squelched Karen's sexual goddess. He became profoundly sorry for forcing his young bride to tolerate his critical mother and deeply regretted his contribution to destroying Karen's sexual radiance. He realized too that for years he had missed out on that joyous part of Karen, which was so important to him.

In the workshop, he wanted to symbolize his desire that they both recover from this negative pattern, so he made Karen a gift of a cactus pad and a rose. From the cactus pad he removed every single thorn, and as he handed it to her, he promised never to wound her sexuality again. The rose? Sam gave it to her commenting on the obvious beauty of such a flower, but with the implicit warning that we must be careful of the thorns that are sometimes attached to the worship of external beauty when internal radiance is unrecognized.

TOOLS FOR ACHIEVING RADIANT LOVEMAKING

The reasons we hide, withdraw, judge, repel, avoid, or lock up our radiance are numerous. Each individual and every couple must look at themselves and explore this area of their relationship to see if the sixth dimension is having trouble. So how do we look at the sixth dimension of our relationship?

By first recognizing the signs of disruption or stress in this dimension, and then through understanding your particular obstacles to accessing your radiance, you can learn how to unleash the beauty, light, and power of the soul. Once you are in touch with your own and each other's soul, then you are in the perfect position to take sex to the next, wondrous dimension, where sex becomes sacred.

1. GOD-GODDESS HALO

Concentrate on the radiance of your partner; see if you can increase it as you are connecting sexually. Practice surrounding him or her with a color, a halo of light, a warmth, and look directly into his or her eyes. Believe that you have an inner radiance and then show it to your lover. Put that halo of light around you, imagine you have a beautiful color emanating from your being, and bestow warmth and beauty upon your lover.

2. THE LOVE ROOM

Create a beautiful place to make love. The sacred is set apart consciously from the mundane, so make a "love room" with candles, incense, music, colors. One woman gleefully reported to me a year after a sexuality consultation of her husband's decision to make a throne of their pool table by putting down a mattress covered with beautiful sheets, buying a circular gauze draping to position over the love nest, and surrounding the area with candles. And she exclaimed, "He's an engineer!"

3. BEAUTY RECOGNITION

Notice one beautiful thing each morning, noon, and night for a week—either in your partner, yourself, your home, your children, or the world outside. Make a point of sharing that observation of beauty with your mate. Draw them into beauty, in all of its forms, and you will share that sensitivity during sex.

4. DISCARD THE CURSE OF PERFECTION, AND ROOT OUT THE HABIT OF CRITICISM

For a day try not to say anything critical! Is it hard, easy, impossible? Then take on an even bigger challenge: try not to think critical thoughts. Pretend that you have a TV broadcasting your thoughts on your forehead and that now you not only have to take responsibility for your actions and words but also for what you are thinking. What a difficult task, but what a difference it would make to adopt that attitude toward the one we love, the one we want to see as a god or goddess.

5. THINK ABOUT AN EXTRAORDINARY SEXUAL EXPERIENCE

If you have one particular lovemaking session in mind, where was your attention? Did you become totally lost in the sensations or were you completely present? Most men and women say their most exceptional sexual experiences occur when they are not focused on themselves, yet they are intensely aware of exquisite feelings being shared. In this dimension, one of our tasks is to relearn the ability to be as unself-conscious as we were as children. It is only as adults that we learn to be aware of how people view us, letting our perceived view of what they see, think, or feel dampen the experience.

6. RECIPROCAL BREATHING: THE NEXT LEVEL OF SOUL GAZING

As we discussed in the heart dimension, one of the most useful tools for building positive energy is "soul gazing," in which a couple hold hands and, without speaking, share how and why they love each other. To take this experience to a more profound level of exchange, a simple alteration of breathing is a delightful adaptation. As you are sitting breathing together with your lover, squeeze her hand lightly as a signal that you are going to hold your next breath while she breathes out. Then when she takes her next breath in, you exhale, sending the breath and energy into her. After a brief pause at the end of the exhale, you are ready to draw in your next breath, and your partner gets to breathe out, filling you with love, energy, and loving purpose. This simple seesaw of breathing is calming, yet it focuses the power of your connection into the giving-and-receiving pattern that affirms the soul connection.

In a meditative sort of way, a couple concentrates on their partner's beauty. This homework is essential for this dimension as well, because it provides a simple ritual for seeing our lover's soul and for allowing our own to be viewed. Within minutes of beginning quiet connection, you may experience tears, smiles, laughter—all expressions of the joy experienced when two souls collide again in love.

Some of the common ways in which people resist soul gazing is by calling it "too woo-woo," complaining that soul gazing sounds too New Age. Others, especially women, immediately claim, "Oh, my partner will never do this" or "We'll start laughing." These reactions reflect a natural nervousness, tied directly to the risk in revealing our radiance: both revealing our radiance and embracing that of our partner is an act of courage.

Looking so steadily and openly into the eyes of your lover can feel scary because it is scary: you can't always

know what you will see in those eyes. When people say
to me, "I'm afraid he or she won't be there to meet me,"
I suggest trying the exercise for a few minutes as a way
of connecting nonverbally. By removing the expectation
of soul gazing's leading directly to sex, the couple may
then have time to get comfortable with each other. But
of course soul gazing may lead to sex, which at this level
of connection, when both souls are open to the other,
can be the vehicle that pushes a couple over the edge
into the transpersonal union of the next dimension.

LET THERE BE AWE

If you've moved through this book charting the waters of your
other five dimensions, reaching the sixth and seventh dimensions is like finding the ultimate sexual oasis. This is the prize,
the promised land that the physical and emotional dimensions
lead to. After you've traveled through your other dimensions,
exploring and mapping them, you are now ready to claim sex in
the spiritual realm.

These final two dimensions contain the gold; they are what
takes good, even powerful sex into the exceptional realm. Here
is where couples who have traveled the road of vulnerability get
to cash in on a sexual relationship that is transformative.

Certainly, a beautiful sunset or a piece of art can help to
trigger our connection to this kind of energy. But more than
likely, we need to unearth and then eliminate some more
potent attitudes or behaviors that prevent us from feeling and
experiencing ourselves as beautiful: the habits of criticism,
vigilance, and self-absorption, the teachings of the sinful nature
of sex.

In each of us, there exists a part that is beyond the usual, and that is our goal: to see this in our partner and cherish it, always. It is up to both partners to realize that real beauty is inside a person, and that the satisfaction one can attain from this level of acceptance and love for another is unendingly deep, providing partners with an enormous reservoir of sensual feelings.

The primary or central challenge of the aesthetic dimension is self-acceptance. By truly embracing who we are, with all of our limitations, flaws, and idiosyncrasies, we not only unlock our radiance, we open ourselves to be embraced by our lover. As such, the aesthetic dimension is the keystone to the doorway of the ecstatic.

When we feel this beauty or radiance in a sexual context, we infuse our connection to our lover with a revitalizing energy, one that surges through us and between us. The ability to gaze into our beloved's eyes and see his or her life, light, and beauty blesses our own soul. When we understand our partner's outer imperfections, but see his or her radiant response to our love-making, we create our own magical aura.

Our task then, sexually, in this dimension is to open ourselves to "seeing" and "being seen" at this depth. In our sexual union the soul is what deepens our connection to our mate or lover. Long ago, before I had even clearly understood the aesthetic dimension, David gave me one of my most treasured compliments. In absolute seriousness with a tremendous smile on his face, he told me, "You light up my life." For me it was a profound moment of his recognition of the exchange of radiance in our relationship.

The combination of the sexual and the spiritual is a path of unending variety as we experience the opening of our lover's soul. Not only does lovemaking in this dimension seem time-less, it has a profound peace and grace that soothes our soul. Now the glances, the touches, the cries of passion, and the soft whispers take us to the unique, to the more than ordinary, and we become open and ready for the most powerful sexual union of all, the transpersonal.

8

The Ultimate Union

THE ECSTATIC PROMISE OF THE
TRANSPERSONAL DIMENSION

*And she felt the soft bud of him within her stirring, and strange rhythms
flushing up into her with a strange rhythmic growing motion, swelling and
swilling till it filled her all cleaving consciousness, and then began again the
unspeakable motion that was not really motion, but pure deepening
whirlpools of sensation swirling deeper and deeper through all her tissue
and consciousness, till she was one perfect concentric fluid of feeling, and
she lay there crying in unconscious inarticulate cries. The voice out of the
uttermost night, the life! The man heard it beneath him with a kind of awe,
as his life sprang out into her.*

—D. H. LAWRENCE, *LADY CHATTERLEY'S LOVER*

ECSTATIC SEX

I consider the sixth and seventh dimensions—the aesthetic
and the transpersonal—the prize for all the energy and
work that sex takes in the preceding dimensions. Perhaps you
are quite satisfied with having your body respond, and you feel
pleasure at infusing your relationship with more lust. However,
if you are willing to experience a transcendent realm of sex,
then I encourage you and your lover to try these final steps to
sacred sex.

Think of it this way: Have you ever made love and felt transported to another realm? To where the rest of the world seems to recede and all that you are aware of is the magic occurring between you and your beloved? To an experience where you are so joined that you have become one, indivisible?

This is a place where you encounter a connection with all that is beyond your individual selves. If you have ever stumbled upon that space, where your two bodies cease to be separate, where you cannot tell where your skin ends and your lover's begins, then you have undoubtedly discovered the place of ecstatic sex. This is the ultimate union: when two become one body, one soul.

This is when sex becomes sacred.

Throughout the ages many poets and mystics have described ecstatic experiences. From the passion of the Sufis to James Joyce's concept of an epiphany, humanity has believed in the concept of ecstasy, of becoming one with someone else, or something larger. The something larger is the divine essence. The very word *ecstasy* is derived from the Latin *ex* or outside and *stasis* or standing. When we have an ecstatic experience, it feels as if we go beyond the boundaries of our physical, emotional self and get in touch with the universe, with God.

You can reach this same kind of transcendent experience through sex. Our culture does not teach us about this potential for sex, and we do not have a form for this divine experience in our society. We have no churches of sexuality, no self-help groups that show us how to make sex spiritual. Instead, sex is shrouded, its glory hidden. Yet I believe this level—where sex becomes spiritual—is what we are ultimately seeking when we make love.

When David and I found this place of spiritual sex, it felt as if I'd discovered a whole new wing of a house that I had lived in for years. We knew that we had experienced ecstatic sex before; in fact, it had happened more than once. Maybe it has happened to you on occasion. But in my case, it seemed almost accidental. I could count on one hand the number of times that I had felt that he and I had become one, when we'd entered into a divine space together. If you were able to discover (or rediscover) your soul as you and your lover worked through the sixth dimension, then you are in a natural place to take this next and final step toward ecstatic, magnificent sex.

You do not have to be either a poet, mystic, or Tantric yogi to experience the profound sexuality of this dimension, but you do have to be open to the belief that this type of spiritual sex is possible, and then you must have the courage to go for it. As you approach claiming this dimension for yourself and your lover, you will need skills so that you can experience the thrill over and over. And as we learn to enter this realm, we need to believe in and embrace sex as a spiritual experience.

ARE YOU READY?

If you believe that ecstatic sex is, at the very least, a possibility, you may now be ready to try to discover the transpersonal dimension for yourself. To identify your own emotional and intellectual tethers that have to be released to fly into this realm, start by responding to the following questions:

1. Do you believe that sex is one path to the sacred experience?
2. Have you ever experienced an ecstatic sexual connection?
3. Are you comfortable with the idea of being a sexual god or goddess?

4. Do you believe that ecstatic sex is possible with your current partner?

5. Do you feel afraid of letting go or surrendering into the sexual experience?

6. Were you taught that sex is wonderful, life affirming, and a way to connect with your partner?

7. Do you practice any type of mindfulness activity: yoga, tai chi, meditation, prayer?

OBSTACLES TO THE ECSTATIC DIMENSION

Since this dimension of sexual connection is so wonderful, since it is so magical and soul expanding, why don't we all believe in it or have it spontaneously? As I've delved deeper into ecstatic lovemaking over the past twelve years and tried to make this experience accessible to many of the men and women who have crossed the threshold of my office, I have discovered powerful cultural blocks to the belief that sex is sacred.

Even if you have already discarded the belief that desire is a sin, as many of us are taught, or were never held back by the belief that sexual lust will lead to the devil, you may still believe that soul sex "just happens." That it is simply, by the grace of God or the Great Spirit, bestowed upon us. We either are lucky or blessed or inexplicably chosen to have it. You either have it or you don't. You picked the right guy or gal or you didn't. Either you are spiritual or you aren't.

If this sounds familiar, then you need to recognize that you are consciously buying into a fatalistic approach to sex, cutting yourself and your beloved off from the possibility that sexual bliss can happen to all of us. By thinking that ecstatic sex only occurs for special couples, you are limiting your own possible experience of sacred sex. Ecstatic sex is a choice that all of us can make if we are willing.

Each situation is unique, but look for the beliefs that keep you from the ecstatic. Challenge those beliefs and begin to exercise your right to sexual bliss. Before taking this final step toward magnificent sex, you will need to identify and clear away any obstacles that may be hindering you from embracing this level of consciousness. These obstacles can be either subtle or obvious, personal or general.

You may be like Wendy and Mike, who had experienced an ecstatic sexual connection with other lovers in the past, but were still negotiating the level of commitment in their relationship to each other. Since their heart dimension (remember the commitment/abandonment dynamic?) was a bit shaky, they did not have the trust in place to take that next step into the unknown. Mike also wanted to see more of Wendy's passion, her lustful and radiant sexuality, but Wendy was afraid to let go until she saw more commitment, more heart, from Mike. As long as they remained in negotiation, they could not fully open their souls. They knew that the transpersonal dimension existed, but they felt distracted by the if-onlys—"If only you will . . . then I will be able to . . ."

Or you may be like Patricia, who after several years of unsuccessful infertility treatments felt defective as a woman. Her biologic dimension had so occupied her approach to sex that she had lost touch with the pleasure dimension and especially with any awareness of herself as a fully sensual, sexual woman. Tim, her husband, was ready to go toward this soulful dimension to heal his wife from all of the medically invasive procedures, but Patricia had to be willing to receive.

As we saw in the sixth dimension, the aesthetic, the fear of losing control, can palpably hamper our ability to release our own radiance and embrace that of our beloved. Cut off from our inner beauty (the place where the soul lives), we cannot let go. The act of letting go is also required for ecstatic sex.

LA PETITE MORT

I find the French word for orgasm very interesting: *la petite mort*, or the little death. Death of what? I believe that it is the death of the ego, that aspect that keeps us separate from our lover. The ego is in charge of me, myself, and I, and protection is its main concern. It is bad enough that we have already asked it to tolerate all of the sharing of the intimacy dimension, it wants no part of this blending baloney! The ego is so concerned with the self that it does not believe that any good comes from ecstasy or "standing outside" of the self. It is fine to have a really passionate experience, even to be radiant and free of self-judgment, but watch out for becoming one with the universe or God. That spells destruction of the ego.

So, as we get closer to melting into our lover's eyes and arms, the ego is liable to set off alarms. It will raise the red flags of "He doesn't really love you," "She can't be trusted," "This is all bull——." It will remind you of the "fact" that none of this sexual ecstasy stuff is really proven, or that you know too much about the past with your partner to be able to see "God" in your lover.

When disbelief or cynicism surfaces, it's difficult to remember the magnificent promise of sacred sex. Can such a marvelous place or thing really exist? Isn't sacred sex just a con, a nice illusion for fools, for those people in woo-woo land? In the beginning, when you are still becoming familiar with this new sexual territory, it is natural to feel awkward and foolish as you approach the sacred realm. We saw this deep-down caution in the heart dimension, when men and women would get stuck in the "game of love," unable to let themselves be openhearted for fear of being hurt, or worse, abandoned. We may feel too over-whelmed by the past, too disconnected to allow sweet surren-der, or too fatigued from our life's responsibilities to engage with our lover at such a deep, thrilling level. So we stay away, deceiving ourselves that we are conserving our emotional energy for other demands. Nothing could be further from the truth! For there is nothing more life enhancing or energy restoring than sacred sex. As was discussed in the sensory and lust dimensions, when we activate our body sexually with a lover, we feel renewed, revitalized, and in this dimension, spiri-tually restored. Letting the ego die during sex doesn't mean the ego nevermore exists, it just is the gateway to the experience of merging with all that is beyond our limited sense of self.

SURRENDER, SURRENDER

There can be no holding back or holding on, because this dimension in its essence is a blending or merging of the two of you. Of course, most of us are understandably hesitant to embrace such a surrender of the self. We have spent most of our lives learning to equate surrender with submission and are therefore bound and determined to stay in control.

Too much dedication to control does not a happy marriage make. And when it comes to sex, a controlling behavior can obstruct the path to our soul. This happened with my husband, David, and me. As a busy, ambitious professional, it is easy for me to get wrapped up in my work. Also, I tend to base a lot of my self-image and self-esteem on my career, and through the years I have kept taking on more and more responsibility. All that responsibility meant there was much more to attend to and to control. Suddenly, I was aware that I had become detached from that inner part of me. David felt that I was absent when we made love and we both felt our sex life had become mechanical. I felt so overwhelmed by the responsibility of juggling all my commitments, I needed to control all aspects of my life, or everything would fall apart. I realized I had become afraid if I let go, even in bed, I'd lose control in all other areas.

This all became clear to me one memorable afternoon. I can still picture the lush mountainside meadow where David and I were taking a long afternoon walk years ago. We were aimless, yet sensually focused, and the beauty of the light on the grasses, the hum of the insects, the smell of the warm earth, led me to see my man in a new way. He became in that instant more beautiful, somehow more exquisite, as I lazily kissed his face where we rested. No hurry. I could trace my love on his face with my lips, and he drank in the elixir of that love. His smile was an opening to his being: there was no worry, no reservation, no carefulness. The more I loved him, the more radiant his being became and the more I glowed as well. The lovemaking that afternoon was done by a new couple—one that had always been there, but one that had been hidden by innumerable cautions. The fusion of our physical and emotional realms had allowed us to enter the spiritual. Once I drew my attention to that place and released my own radiance, I was able to reconnect with David in a new, more profound way. It is memories of afternoons such as that one that continue to make me hungry to taste the sweet pleasure of ecstatic sex again and again.

David and I are not alone in our discovery of magnificent sex. Annamarie and Leonardo came back a few days after their initial visit with me, during which we discussed ways for them to bring life back to their sexual encounters. I had given them the healing massage exercise (described in chapter 9), and they had a wonderful experience when Annamarie was receiving and Leonardo was giving. Annamarie completely let go into Leonardo's loving touch and into his stimulation of her sacred (G) spot. She was powerfully orgasmic and Leonardo was thrilled.

The difficulty, they said, came the next night when Leonardo was the receiver and Annamarie the giver. He described being anxious and nervous. He was unable to get an erection and stopped her pleasuring of his body after a few minutes. Annamarie knew the experience had been difficult and awkward, but she did not know how to help Leonardo receive pleasure.

As we discussed this experience that had puzzled them, Leonardo realized his anxiety was about losing control. He had never (never!) just received pleasure during sex. He was usually so focused on his wife that even though he enjoyed sex tremendously, he had not understood how much he disassociated from his own sensual experience. He was immersed in performance goals, in the job he had to do to his wife to prove that he was a good lover. He was afraid of his emotional reaction if he surrendered to his wife. He might cry, he might yell, he didn't know what might happen, and until this exercise, he had had no idea of how completely he had avoided vulnerability during sex.

Both Annamarie and Leonardo came from South America, and since their native language was Spanish, I pulled out my book of poetry by Pablo Neruda, full of the incredible passion and pleasure in a love relationship. After we read some of the beautiful language, there was electricity in the air. I then asked Leonardo two questions: If now was not the time to surrender, then when? And if he was not going to surrender to Annamarie, then to whom?

As they left the session, both Leonardo and Annamarie became excited about exploring sexual surrender in order to create a new sexual crucible for their well-aged marriage. They decided to begin reading erotic poetry to each other, to practice soul gazing and reciprocal breathing daily, and to consciously look for the god and goddess in each other.

Sexual surrender is not easy. Some men and women have told me that when they get to this point in lovemaking, they feel as if they might disappear. At some basic level the experience becomes so overwhelming they worry they will not be able to come back to their "normal" state. Yet in all my experience personally and professionally, I have never heard of someone who was left out in the void because of such a powerful sexual fusion.

STAYING IN TOUCH WITH YOUR SACRED ENERGY

Many women and men do not enter the spiritual sexual realm because they believe that sacred sex is too hard to achieve. They are dissuaded by the belief that accessing the sacred in our daily, "normal" life is impossible because of the four D's: deadlines, dishes, diapers, or our routine daily tasks. They assume that any activity requiring so much intense energy must also require time and work—and who has that to spare? They feel that they'd have to give up their job, learn how to meditate, or become a Tantrica and dance around the house naked! Otherwise, it just wouldn't happen. And since we are barely able to fit a "quickie" into the week's schedule, how in the world are we going to have time for long, prolonged, exquisite lovemaking sessions?

Barb and Lou had plenty of deadlines. They lived in San Francisco as a young, career-oriented couple. As they became more successful at their jobs, they became less successful sexually. There were no long walks in Golden Gate Park as there had been; there were no sensual Saturday mornings anymore because usually one of them had to go in to the office "just for a couple of hours." Barb's goddess energy was buried under a pile of papers, and Lou was too stressed to see and acknowledge it anyway. He certainly did not feel like a sexual god. For this couple a serious look at their priorities was in order. They had to clear a path to one another through the jungle of their business lives to reencounter the ecstatic. Now, that is a hidden treasure worth bushwhacking for!

Another woman, Shirley, had the dishes and diapers problem. Like so many women, she was exhausted by the unending demands of her household and the physical clinging of her small children. She informed me that she was very organized and did manage to nurture her toddlers as well as to "get it all done." She even squeezed in the time to volunteer at her older children's school in the sexuality program. But when it came to her own vibrant sexual connection, Shirley admitted ruefully that she got an F. She knew that there was a place where spirituality and sexuality existed together, and in the past, she and her husband had treasured those "odd but glorious moments." But now she no longer had the energy even to try to rediscover that place. There was some resentment on Shirley's part—not at her children, but at the incredible demands of motherhood. Her sensuality seemed a distant memory, and when her husband came up behind her at the sink, she was more likely to twist out of his hug than to snuggle into his body. She was too busy and too irritable for the sensual exchange.

The lack of connection to her goddess energy was threatening to make Shirley a bitter woman. When I told her that directly, tears welled up in her eyes. "I know," she said, "I can almost feel it happening." We had another long discussion after she had had a few days to digest the choices she had made in her life with her mate. She had called her man in the meantime and talked into the night about what had happened to the profound sexual love they used to enjoy. Shirley had opened the box of sexual detachment and dared to look inside. She decided to reawaken the goddess, and that meant putting some limits on her totally consuming role of motherhood. In Shirley's case she was ready, she needed that part of her being. She already had a new glow about her as she anticipated her homecoming from her delighted and somewhat stunned husband.

Sacred sexual exchange is a vast container that requires the giver to function as a healer, as someone who awakens his or her partner, and also as a receiver of joy. These three actions—healing, awakening, and receiving—are the essence of how the lover and the beloved interact. To have this lover/beloved connection we must believe that we can be a healer of our beloved. If you have lived with your own and others' addictions, for example, you may be very aware of the limitations on healing another person. In fact, many of us have been codependent with someone who has not been able to face his or her demons. However, this does not mean that our emotional and physical loving does not have a healing essence. We can extend compassion, kindness, and forgiveness, and when we do, we are healers. The shift takes place when we begin to do this during the sexual encounter, when we consciously use the sexual energy to heal our partner's prior experience or negative teaching about sex. Remember the woman who held her partner's balls after his long, hard day at work? She did that only half in jest because she did believe that sexual energy heals many wounds. We do heal our lover with our sexual energy when it is given freely without demanding a return.

TOOLS FOR ACCESSING ECSTATIC SEX

As I promised, there are several practical, tangible tools for accessing this dimension.

1. FOCUS YOUR ATTENTION

This first group of practices helps to strengthen your ability to focus your attention, which is necessary for being present to the sexual experience, for ensuring conscious loving. The good news is that great, ecstatic sex does not have to take any longer than mediocre sex. In fact, once some of the focusing techniques are learned and practiced, arousal, lubrication, and wonderful passion are accessed much faster and with much more ease than before. Becoming skilled at managing your thought distractions not only helps us in business and in learning, but also in connecting sexually.

Meditation
There are many excellent ways to learn meditation. There are classes on yoga meditation, on quiet meditation, on prayer as meditation. The skills that are useful are the abilities to quiet all the chatter in our heads, to rebalance our autonomic nervous system as was described in the heart dimension, and to experience a sense of calmness. No longer is meditation an "out there" technique; it is being taught in hospitals throughout the country as a healing tool, and it is helpful in connecting us to our center, to our essence. You may not want to engage in a formal class, but schedule some time for this type of activity every day, even if it is a meditative walk. Being able to share your essence sexually requires that you have a connection to that essence.

Mindfulness

Mindfulness is a close cousin to meditation. It is also a skill that involves paying attention. Every day we are paying attention to what matters to us; we are mindful of what counts. Sexually, we can focus on our lover, become mindful of this partner and aware of his or her presence in our life, in our house, in the very room we occupy often unconsciously. When we know the dimensions our partner is strong in, we can use that awareness to connect. If our beloved is a romantic, strong in the heart dimension, then we bring home flowers, surprise gifts, a poem or a card, tokens of our commitment. If our partner is very positive about the desire or lust aspect, we can "spring" sex on him or her in an unlikely place or at an unusual time, seducing him or her with our passion. Mindfulness also means feeding the sexual stream that runs between you and your lover. It means taking time to connect sensually and not to let the drudgery of every day tarnish the sexual chalice.

Soul Gazing

Do not forget soul gazing. Although you learned this in the heart and aesthetic dimensions, bringing the soul into sex is the transformative pivot. Practice soul gazing at least once a day for a week, even if it is just for a few minutes. You will notice a difference. Strike an agreement with your partner that you will begin at least four lovemaking sessions with soul gazing to consciously bring this level of connection to the two of you right at the beginning of sex. For me, the soul gazing practice was revolutionary because it not only provided the form, the ritual, for exchanging love with David, but also showed me how to get rid of distractions to that flow of energy during sex. I have a busy mind. I have been known to make lists of my lists, and even to add things that I have already done to my list just for the pleasure of crossing them off! As you might imagine, I get a lot done, but there is a price to pay. I may not be fully in the moment, fully present for the experience at hand. Many of us have this habit. So, even if we want to open our hearts and souls to our partner, we get sidetracked by the details of life's lists.

2. OPENING THE HEART AND SOUL

Now that you have focused your attention on your connection to your inner self, your beloved, and your sexual connection, the next task is to open your heart. You can be an accomplished meditator, a person mindful of the moment, and someone who sits opposite their partner holding hands, but that does not necessarily mean that you have opened your heart or soul. The first step is of course to have the desire to open to your lover; the next is to have ways to overcome your resistance to doing so. I know that you have looked at the resistances, cultural or personal, so now begin to attack the habit of hiding your soul.

Imagery

Imagine your heart and soul as having a shape and a location. Most people put the soul in the chest, and of course we know that our heart belongs there, so give them a shape and a color and a texture, and then imagine this heart, this soul, opening to your beloved. See them as energy transmitters, as powerful generators of a healing force, and send that beam of love to your partner often, many times a day, over the phone, in person, and across the room. Be especially aware of doing this when you are soul gazing, and then be open to receiving. Remember that can be the most difficult task, as Leonardo, the South American businessman, found out to his surprise. But imagery can help establish this connection between the two of you as a bridge to the ecstatic. Even if you practice this imagery of the open heart during your day-to-day travels, I can guarantee you that something different will happen, someone else will open their heart to you. It is a powerful tool at any time, and it is incredible during sex.

Conscious Kiss

Try this kissing experiment: Kiss your mate as if you are mad or at least annoyed at him or her. Next, kiss your lover as if he or she is trying to make up but you are not ready to yet. Finally, kiss your lover in a way to indicate that you would like it to lead to more. You can do this, right? We all know how to express volumes of information with a single kiss. And we all kiss unconsciously, a "Bye, honey, have a nice day" or a "Hello, I'm home" kiss. But it is wonderful to make kissing conscious. You can not only put emotional content into the kiss, you can play with your lover by tugging his or her bottom lip, sucking at the soft skin, barely whispering across the little folds of his or her mouth. In other words, the kiss becomes conscious, it becomes an experience that you only share with this one person; it is not a mommy kiss or a friend kiss or a daughter kiss. It is a lover's kiss, a heart-to-heart, soul-to-soul kiss that reminds you both of this dimension in an instant. We need reminding to keep the duties, diapers, dishes, deadlines— those four D's—at bay.

Practice Seeing God in One Another

God, Spirit, Higher Self, exists in all of us; we are not used to the idea of making love to that self. Having sex with the Divine, or the Beloved, may not only seem sacrilegious, but impossible. And yet as we gaze on the radiant face of our lover, as we receive the honor of revelation from our partner, we connect with God in them. Once a day for the next week or two, practice seeing God in this way. Pause when you are reading together in the same room and *look* at your mate; after a conscious kiss, watch for the Beloved to appear. It is always there of course in both of you; the joy is in the recognition. As you become more adept at seeing the Spirit, you will find this powerful energy with you as you join bodies.

THE PATH TO BLISS IS YOURS

Does every other dimension have to be absolutely perfect for this experience to be realized? Do you have to be near sainthood for sex to take on this quality? No, but you do have to look for blocks in the first six dimensions that prevent combining passion with spirit. Like any path of personal growth, accessing and achieving ecstatic sex requires skill through practice. Sex, the "wellspring" of your relationship, requires diligent attention and nurturing. You and your partner need to commit to this kind of connection and practice it regularly.

The transpersonal dimension is about lovemaking in its most profound sense. It is about ecstasy, sexual ecstasy, the experience we all long for in a full, deep, passionate connection with our beloved. This is about making love with our partner and having it take our breath away. This is lovemaking that changes the quality of light in the room, the face of your beloved, the entire nature of your existence. Lovemaking in the seventh dimension has the quality of the sacred, of reaching beyond ourselves to a place of connection where we see the essence of ourselves connecting with that of our partner.

In the next chapter I offer a practical, step-by-step way of accessing the ecstatic: it is called Tantric sex. This is the mind-blowing discovery David and I made together that has trans-formed our relationship. Though Tantra may not be for everybody, I can say without reservation that my husband and I have found it to be a guaranteed way of reaching ecstatic sex. I encourage you to try, to reach, to break beyond the boundaries. After all, you deserve it.

9

The Tantric Way

A PROVEN PATH TO THE SACRED

ONE MORE CHALLENGE

I f you believe that ecstatic sex is possible, then I want to offer you a further way of accessing this realm of the sacred. But first I want to share a personal story.

David and I were absolutely equal in our lives before we encountered Tantra, and we still are to a great extent. However, then everything was based on our desire to be fair to one another. In a curious way, there was little to distinguish us as male and female. We had met in medical school, took the same courses, graduated at the same time, and went to the same residency training. We both cooked, cleaned, and cared for our house and possessions. We took turns shopping at the grocery store; one year in our medical practice we each billed out a total year's earnings within $200 of each other. We adopted our two children so there wasn't even the experience of pregnancy and nursing to separate us. Obviously, we each had our own personality, and mine was more people-oriented and David's more intellectual, but we were dedicated to equality and fairness in our relationship. As I have said before, we had good sex, it was fun, orgasmic, and it was getting a bit stale, but nothing that we felt was a problem.

Then a couple, best friends of ours, called us after they had gone to a workshop in Hawaii on Tantric loving for couples, led by Charles and Caroline Muir. They felt that it had transformed their relationship. They said that we *had* to go and do the workshop ourselves, and furthermore, the next workshop was in six weeks. I replied that there was no way we could go to Hawaii in six weeks; we had already planned a ski trip for our vacation. But David looked at me and then said, "Hawaii? Sex? I'm sure we could arrange to go!"

That trip to Hawaii was the beginning for us of a long journey into ecstatic sex that continues to this day. What we found in Tantra was a container or, more appropriately, a chalice for David and me to share an ecstatic experience. By harnessing all the energy of the six other dimensions (our passion, our love for one another, our lust, our attraction, our intimacy, and our radiance), we took our connection to a higher, more potent level through sex. And although Tantra is not the only way to experience sacred sex, I have found that it provides concrete tools and steps that take the guesswork out of reaching this ultimate, profound level.

Tantra, which is an elaborate yoga system developed in ancient India three thousand years ago, teaches that sexual practice is a path to the ultimate connection with all living things, but especially to the Beloved in your partner, to the Divine. For the original Tantric yogis, it was a path to enlightenment for the ordinary man and woman. Unlike other forms of meditation and paths to spiritual enlightenment that were reserved for high holy priests or monks, Tantra was accessible in an everyday kind of way. Tantric sex is first and foremost about discovering a path or making a journey to the sacred through sex, and it was an entire way of life in India three thousand years ago. In presenting and encouraging you to consider this belief system, I do not feel that you need to adopt a whole new religion. But couldn't we borrow a few ideas of theirs that would expand our concept of sex?

David and I are not alone in using this ancient system as a path to sexual bliss. Recently, there has been a wave of interest in this belief system precisely because lovers want to experience a transformation of souls. Learning Tantra has not only made ecstatic sex possible, it has made it probable. We now know that we can depend on the skills we have achieved through this approach to take us to this exquisite place over and over and over again and we have taught this to countless other couples. It has become the single most important event in our relationship, one that has forever altered us as both individuals and a couple. It has endured and helped us through all of life's other challenges.

TANTRA, THE BASICS

Although I have vastly simplified Tantra for you, it is in fact an elaborate yoga that's about more than just sex. It contains sixty-five other arts that Tantricas believe will lead you to enlightenment, including flower arranging, tattooing, gardening, and war. The resource section lists several books, as well as videos of couples practicing sexual Tantra, for those of you who wish to study this powerful path. However, for our purposes, the important concept is that sex is a *way* to the sacred, to nirvana, to heaven. For the practitioners of Tantra, sex is the upward-spiraling blending of male and female sexual energies; it is the transpersonal dimension. The skills of engaging this energy need to be studied and practiced as seriously as you would those of any other endeavor that you wanted to master. But this is the most delightful and engaging course of study that you will ever undertake!

I have included several practical techniques for accessing and integrating Tantric exercises into your sex life. More important are the profound changes—fundamental shifts in attitudes and beliefs about love—couples will experience if they have the courage to start this sexual adventure toward the ecstatic. If you decide to begin these exercises, you and your mate will begin to

▶ Feel sex as an exchange of energy to heighten awareness and experience, rather than as a discharge of energy or a way to reduce tension

▶ See sex as a path to enlightenment or personal growth, rather than a commodity to give or get

▶ Experience sex as the practice of a sacred ritual, rather than an isolated or spontaneous event that has no meaning beyond the act itself or the goal of orgasm

▶ Allow sex to be a direct link to the Divine, rather than a mundane, bodily act

For you to experience these ideas as real and tangible, they have to be practiced. You and your lover have to be open and willing to feel these ideas in your hearts, bones, and souls. In general, you need to begin to approach sex as an exchange of energy, remaining conscious and aware during all aspects. This requires skill and practice in the use of attention, perception, and consciousness—all of the skills that we learned about in the transpersonal dimension. But you can do it the way many couples have in our workshops. Here are some of the basic ideas that support this wonderful lovemaking.

The central concepts of Tantra are based upon the idea of energy exchange. The Tantric yogis see the universe as made up of a dance of two sources of energy, the female and the male. In essence, energy works off of two extremes, or poles. You may be familiar with the terms *yin* and *yang*. Like those two essential aspects of a whole, Tantra expresses two opposing but necessary forces as deities (or sources of energy), the Shiva and the Shakti. Though Tantra does not make a strict division between male and female, the archetypal associations with Shiva tend to be masculine (light, hard, active, analytical) and the associations with Shakti tend to be feminine (dark, soft, receptive, intuitive). Since every thing, every action, contains these dual forces or energies, the key to harmony or power is to create the conditions for both energies to flow. Sexually, it's the two together, the Shiva and the Shakti, that allows for the ultimate form of harmony: a union that transcends. That is of course where we are during the sexual exchange.

Essentially, three things are happening between a man and a woman during Tantric sex:

▶ The woman (Shakti) is the source of powerful, creative energy. But for the sexual energy to be awakened, the man (Shiva) needs to ignite her goddess energy.

▶ The woman has an infinite reservoir of that sexual energy that she can tap into and release, whereas the man's energy source is more fragile and can be depleted. This is why one of the main exercises in Tantra for the man is the practice of ejaculatory control and learning to have an orgasm without ejaculating. He needs to help the woman build sexual tension and not discharge his too soon.

▶ When the woman accepts being a goddess sexually with a tremendous reservoir of energy, and when the man devotes himself to nourishing his goddess, he benefits and receives energy as her sexual energy is activated. He is charged up with her powerful force.

To approach the transpersonal, we have to accept not only that this dimension is possible sexually, but also that we can claim it. And actually, it is fun! Becoming a sexual goddess is a wonderful, delightful aspect of the feminine that most women do not get to experience often. I certainly realized that my goddess was left far behind as I went to medical school and became a doctor. This happens to so many of us who are competing in the male world. And, on the other hand, most men love the idea of being a sexual god and they absolutely beam when I tell them that the Tantra term for the penis is *vajra,* meaning "thunder bolt," or *lingam,* meaning "wand of light"! (Men always want their penises to be light sabers anyway.) So, even though the "sacred" has the aura of seriousness for most of us raised in Western religions, we can have a light, joyful approach to this dimension.

Now you need to learn some of the techniques that will help you bring this special sex into your relationship. It is time to create your own mini sexual workshop. As I have said, it will take openness, exploration, and a willingness to tolerate a bit of uncertainty or awkwardness as you and your partner learn something new, but the payoff is big!

TECHNIQUES TO PRACTICE FOR TANTRIC SEX

HEALING MASSAGE

This technique taught me how much control I had to have with sex. The instructions are simple: you and your partner set up two sexual, sensual pleasuring sessions on consecutive days.

First, perhaps you will pleasure him. As is described in detail below in the Conscious Loving program, you want to provide a languorous, sense-filled thirty to sixty minutes with the intent of allowing him to completely let go into the experience. You will bring him to the point of orgasm several times and then back off, prolonging the experience before allowing him to ejaculate. You will intend during your touch of him to heal any and all bad feelings or experiences he has had sexually. You will pour your love into him and be his love goddess. And you will not have intercourse because that will then change the experience into one of his "doing you." This experience is a one-way gift.

Later that day or evening you can have intercourse if you must, but this experience will be reversed the next day with him giving to you in the same fashion. *No* intercourse. In our sexuality workshop we assign the men to pleasure their woman first. In our experience the love and attention extended by the men toward their woman are the keys to her feeling loved and appreciated, which unlocks the sexual passion.

At first when David and I received this seemingly simple, delightful assignment, I was afraid to just lie there and receive. I felt more than naked as David gazed lovingly into my eyes while he was touching my sacred *yoni* (vagina) and G spot. I wanted to do him back because then I would be back in control. It is that old surrender thing again. However, once you experience the bliss of truly letting go into this fabulous sexual space, you'll want to do it again and again.

EJACULATORY CONTROL

By learning to orgasm without ejaculation, a Tantric and Taoist (from China) practice, men can enhance their own and their partner's sexual pleasure. Now, I know this is hard to believe, conditioned as we are to define orgasm as ejaculation, but it is not only possible, it is immensely pleasurable. A man can make love every day or every other day, satisfying his partner and enjoying peaks of sensation without ejaculating.

Ejaculation in both Tantric and Taoist systems is thought of as depleting the energy. What man has not experienced the deep need to sleep after coming? Besides possibly inciting the wrath of his partner, who views her partner's sudden exhaustion as "loving and leaving" her, a man frequently loses his sexual charge entirely. Tantric and Taoist texts have suggested that ejaculating every fourth or seventh time slowly builds sexual energy which can be used in the outside world—in business, other physical pursuits, or accomplishing other goals. Although you may not want to wait for days to ejaculate, developing this ability to orgasm separately from releasing semen can be a wonderful skill. It allows you to avoid the refractory period where another erection or ejaculation is impossible, a valuable technique as one ages, which makes satisfying your woman much easier, as well. But most of all, it prolongs and intensifies your pleasure.

How to do this? Begin by telling your partner that you want to try this technique. (She may think there is something drastically wrong if you don't come in the usual way.) Then approach orgasm, but back away the moment before you climax. To back off, squeeze your PC muscles (see biologic chapter). Do this several times, and enlist your partner's help by having her stop stimulation for the moment. Pay attention to your sensations and especially to your breathing. Take slow belly breaths, and relax the muscles of your back, legs, and abdomen. Again use your PC muscles to control the urge to release genitally. Instead, focus your attention and energy up to your head, and then out your fingers and toes. Vavoom! A whole-body orgasm and you are still ready to go on! This peak experience may not happen the first time you try this technique, but it is definitely worth practicing.

The key concepts are relaxing and spreading the energy throughout your body. When you want, you can decide to orgasm with an ejaculation. This charging of the power center is a wonderful enhancement of the desire dimension, one your partner can share in and enjoy as you learn to build and control sexual energy.

THREE CEREMONIES TO TRY AT HOME

In our "Sex: Body and Soul" workshop for couples, David and I have developed three crucial ceremonies for couples to integrate Tantra practices into their sexual repertoire. They are based on several of the Tantra techniques already described, blending them into one long lovemaking session. They incorporate the healing massage exercise discussed above, but they are consciously multidimensional. If you and your lover are game to try something new, schedule time for this experience on an upcoming weekend. Many couples have found an entirely new way of connecting sexually after these sessions.

The first ceremony asks for the man to be the primary giver, the woman the receiver. In the second session, the man is the receiver, while the woman is the giver. You need to do both "homework assignments"; one alone does not provide balance. In a way, you are taking apart the sexual experience. Then there will be a joint session to put it all back together in a new way. Try all of these and I promise they will open the door to sacred loving for you and your lover!

CONNECTING SACRED ENERGIES
Man Giving—Woman Receiving

Purpose: This is a ceremony in which the man activates
his woman's goddess energy (Shakti). He knows that
connecting with her Shakti will energize him as well.
Her sacred sexual energy is the wellspring of their
relationship, and his role is to awaken it for the benefit
of both.

Setting: The man creates a sacred space in which to bring
forth his goddess's energy. He arranges this space with
care and attention to detail, evoking as many of the senses
as possible. Think about lighting, music, scent, arrangement of pillows and bedclothes. The TV should not only
be off but covered. I cannot emphasize enough how
important this step is. Women comment all the time how
special it was to them that their partner took the trouble
to create a beautiful space for their lovemaking session. It
indicates that her man cares about the details of what is
pleasing to her and is willing to take time to show his love
and caring.

Preparation: The man sends his woman off to bathe while
he prepares the space as above. He should have available
massage oil or lotion and personal lubricant (remember
Astroglide?). Towels should be placed under his beloved.
He should prepare himself appropriately to honor a goddess: face shaved, nails clipped, attractively dressed, clean,
and perhaps scented. Mental preparation is even more
important: a calm, loving attitude with a sense of devotion
should be cultivated.

Invitation: When your woman emerges from her bath, welcome her with your smile and invite her to the prepared bed. Be sure to maintain loving eye contact.

Soul gazing: Sit across from one another holding hands and breathe together, maintaining eye contact. Visualize a flow of energy between you with each breath. This is your chance to pour loving energy into her as you look into her eyes. For now, do not talk but flood her with loving thoughts.

Touching: Invite her to recline on the bed. Begin to touch her gently, perhaps on the face. Move to other parts of her slowly and attentively. Use oil or lotion if you like. Talk to her: tell her about her skin, her hair, her eyes, how it makes you feel to touch her. Kiss her, use your lips on many parts of her. Do this without expectation of response; she is to simply receive your attention. Welcome any show of emotion from her.

Heart center: Maintain an awareness of your heart center as you touch your beloved. Feel your loving energy flow out through your hands and lips to her; imagine that she is soaking it up. Visualize her heart growing with your attention. Connect your hand to her heart for a while and breathe together, soul gazing.

Sacred spot: After spending plenty of time in gentle exploration of her face, arms, legs, belly, and breasts, bring your attention to her yoni. Sitting to the side of your beloved will allow you to maintain close connection with her, keeping a soft, gentle focus of love and appreciation in your eyes and words, with an awareness of heart-to-heart connection. Begin to explore the soft folds of the outer part of the yoni with one hand; the other hand might rest on her heart or belly. Use lubricant as needed. Ask her permission to enter her sacred space with your finger, and once it is given, do so gently and slowly. Make contact with the sacred spot, on the roof of the yoni under the pubic bone, with the utmost care. Begin to coax it with gentle strokes, pausing often. If you are attentive, you may be able to feel a current of energy running between you when you pause. Many variations in pressure, pace, and direction of stroke are possible. You might place your thumb on the clitoris lightly. Let your goddess's responses guide you; remember that there is no goal of orgasm, only of pleasure and connection. Remember to look into her eyes and breathe with her. If she wants to make sounds, encourage this, and sound with her. Smile!

Duration: Continue your loving attention to the sacred spot for many minutes, resting whenever needed by either of you. Many emotions may arise during your connection. Try to stay with them, feel them in your body, and breathe through them, and encourage her to do the same; don't process or analyze them now. Energy may build and release through several cycles. Often the experience is not the familiar one of sexual arousal and release to which the two of you have become accustomed, but rather something very different. Laughing and crying are not uncommon forms of energy release; even angry outbursts may occur. Simply observe, be present, honor, share, breathe, and do not judge.

Amrita: Your woman may experience release of a fluid during sacred spot connection, known in Tantra as *amrita*. This is the female ejaculate we discussed in the biologic dimension and it is quite natural. Often there is a considerable quantity (hence the towels). It is a thin fluid and is expelled from the urethra, but it is not urine. Its release does not necessarily occur during a typical orgasm, although it is usually associated with an energetic release. *Amrita* should be welcomed as a special blessing, but it is perfectly okay if it is not released.

Finishing: Conclude your connection with a gentle embrace with full body contact. You may be highly aroused, but this is not the time for intercourse. Simply absorb the energy by breathing it up, and allow it to spread throughout your body. Be aware of your beloved's glow. Let her know in words how you felt when you received her Shakti. Spend some time in silence as well.

CONNECTING SACRED ENERGIES
Woman Giving—Man Receiving

Purpose: As with the woman receiving, this is a ceremony to honor the male energy (Shiva). The woman may have a sense that her man doubts his energy or his sexual skill or even his anatomy. Because there is so much emphasis on performance for the male, both his and hers, rarely do men allow themselves to just receive. The purpose for the woman is to reawaken her man to pure pleasure, to the world of sensation, and to play with his sexual arousal.

Setting: Creating the proper space for this ceremony is important and wonderfully creative. As you attend to all the senses—sight, sound, touch, taste, smell, and movement—let your imagination loose. Hang scarves over lights, find exciting and/or soothing music, put your perfume on the pillow, ensure that there will be no interruptions, and make the bed a throne. Place towels on the bed if you want to use oils. Consider flowers beside the bed. Have fruit juices to drink during your pleasure session.

Preparation: Send your man off to bathe while you make the preparations. You may want to have lotion or oil to massage his body. You will want to be radiant yourself, clean, scented, dressed in something easy and flowing, or in nothing but a scarf and earrings! As you await your beloved, think about why you want to pleasure him, and adopt an attitude of creating joy in him.

Invitation: When your lover emerges, greet him with your smiling face and lead him to the waiting bed. Perhaps dance with him along the way. Send him appreciation with your eyes.

Soul gazing: Sit across from one another holding hands and breathe together. Imagine seeing into the heart of this man and allow him to see into yours. With each breath imagine sending him loving energy.

Touching: Invite him to lie back on the pillows. Begin to touch his face, his head, and his neck, spending time on each feature as if you were going to memorize his visage with your hands. You may use your lips, your hair, and your breasts as well as you slowly explore all of his body. Use lotion or oil if you like, hum or whisper love words, tantalize every part of his physical being. Encourage him to let all of this loving in. No response is expected or even desired. If he gets an erection, fine. If not, fine. If he gets one and it goes away, fine, because there will be no intercourse.

Heart center: As you touch this wonderful person, stay connected with your heart. Imagine that your heart sends radiant energy through your body to him. Imagine that you are turning him on in the most profound sense. Keep connected to his eyes, do not let him sleep, but let him be both at ease and aroused.

Lingam and scrotum: When you feel ready to touch this wand of light, do so with the utmost love. Most men have not had their lingam really loved. Spend time with the shaft and base, but even more time with the tip and its rounded ridge. Carefully explore the V with gentle fingertips or lips. Move the skin firmly and lovingly along the shaft. Explore the scrotum and testicles with varying touch. Caress and massage the part of the lingam under and behind the scrotum in the perineum too. There is a lot to play with, and you have plenty of time. Remember to stay connected with eyes and heart; it is good to speak words of love and desire too.

Ejaculatory control: Allow your man to build energy, but help him to contain the energy and spread it throughout himself, rather than striving for orgasm and ejaculation.

Watch him and stay connected to his experience. Encourage him to express to you how close he is to orgasm. Ask him to ride the edge of pleasure and to experiment with taking the energy to several peaks and backing away from the release. In this fashion, he might even have a kind of orgasmic experience without ejaculation. You can help him control his ejaculation by stopping any stimulation and applying firm pressure in the perineum behind the scrotum until the energy dissipates a bit. Remind him to breathe deeply, to relax his muscles, and to imagine the energy flowing upward along the spine to the heart and head. After several peaks, you and he may decide to experience a conscious ejaculation. If and when he comes, stay connected with eye contact and awareness of heart connection; sound out with him. Welcome his fluid; play with the silken liquid before you gently remove it with a cloth. Alternatively, you may decide together to finish the connection without ejaculation, which might be a new experience for both of you.

Duration: Be aware of the tendency to hurry to a climax. Allow yourself and your man to float in the pleasure experience. He may be overwhelmed by the experience of true giving from you, he may cry, he may shout and laugh, he may be sad or angry as he recalls past sexual experiences that were humiliating or even shameful. Welcome all emotion. Breathe, stay focused on your beloved, and keep pouring love into him. Demand nothing.

Finishing: Conclude the connection of your sacred energies with a warm embrace and full body contact. Remember, no matter how sexually aroused you may have become, or he has become, there is no intercourse. Take in the energy through your breath, your heart, and your eyes. Bathe in the radiance of your beloved. Tell him what it was like to be his goddess, and to pleasure him. Leave him to rest and to absorb the healing experience.

Once you have experienced both the giving and receiving aspects separately, you will want to put all of this together. Do this delicately, consciously, because the tendency will be to fall back into your old habits. Imagine that this is the *first* time you have made love to this man or woman; treat him or her as if he or she is a precious virgin to the ultimate love experience.

LOVE IN SEVEN DIMENSIONS
A Combined Program for You and Your Lover

Setting and preparation: Prepare the bedroom together. Again, think of all the senses. One of you may prepare taste treats, the other the music and the lighting. Make sure everything smells delicious and that all your oils and lubricants are within easy reach. Agree on general task division—but surprise each other with specifics. Remember your generous heart as you make these preparations. Then take a bath or shower together. Make this a water experience where you explore and groom one another. Make it sensuous, fun, and caring. Perhaps you will want to put on some music just for the bath that suits the mood.

Invitation: Play touch hands—naked!—for a while. Tune in to your lover's energy, adapt to it, flow with it—and show your own energy openly, generously, and joyfully. Have fun as you move with one another, first one leading and then the other and finally blending into leaderless motion. Finish with a thank-you bow to your lover and move on to your bed.

Soul gazing: Sit across from one another on the bed—use pillows under your bottom for comfort—and soul gaze. Take your time, there is absolutely no reason to hurry this sacred connection. Begin by harmonizing your breathing first (i.e., breathe in and out at the same time). Then change to reciprocal breathing (he breathes in while she breathes out and vice versa). Visualize a current of energy—or a color or a magic fluid—circulating between you, out your right hand and into your lover's heart on the outbreath, in through your left hand and into your heart on the inbreath. It is wonderful to imagine pouring energy into your mate, but remember to receive into your open heart as well.

Touching: After a suitable interval, the goddess reclines, and her man begins to pleasure her gently and sensually (as in the first homework exercise). Touch/massage all over the body at first, with gradually more attention to her outer yoni lips and clitoris, using plenty of lubrication. Gentlemen, be teasing, and wait for an invitation to enter the yoni with your fingers. Here is your opportunity to use your knowledge of your goddess and what awakens her Shakti. Continue to expand your knowledge of this most important of all subjects by being open and receptive to her suggestions, both verbal and nonverbal. A lifelong project! Don't forget all the different kinds of touch and stroking that are possible, and provide plenty of variation. Remember the two poles of her sexual center and their different qualities: yang at the clitoris, yin at the sacred spot.

Goddess, receive his attention and touch, concentrating on remaining open in your heart and yoni and connected with your lover. He may wish to place one hand on your heart to help you connect it with your yoni. Together you would again imagine or visualize a flow of energy: this time from his heart out through his hand into your yoni, up to your heart, back through his other hand to his heart. You should feel free to move, make noise, talk to him, or whatever you would like to build your sexual energy. Orgasm, should it occur now, is perfectly appropriate— but not required!

Reciprocating: At some point you will want to exchange roles, the goddess now pleasuring her god. All the advice of the preceding paragraph applies. Men, you are building your energy—but remember to stay relaxed and to spread it out throughout your body. Women, you can help him with this by staying tuned in to his level of arousal (verbally and nonverbally), using both poles of his genital center (tip of lingam is yang, perineum is yin), and stroking him with a free hand out toward his extremities and up to his head from time to time. Both of you need to stay connected, remember to breathe, and visualize the flow of energy between you. Keep your eyes open, be radiant, and see the radiance in your lover! (You will probably want to defer orgasm at this point, unless you already know how to have one without ejaculating.)

Joining: By now you are probably ready for the lingam to enter the yoni. This is a special and powerful moment. Honor it with full eye contact to acknowledge your trust in one another, your complete heart openness, and full soulfulness. Take your time and savor the moment, perhaps with some simple stillness at first. Then you can begin to play with your energies together, using touch hands. Try different rhythms, different depths and directions of thrust. (One especially arousing pattern is for him to stroke light and shallow for four or five strokes, then once deep, then repeat a number of times.) Try some different positions, especially Yab Yum if you can do it comfortably. In Yab Yum the woman sits facing her partner, either in his lap or between his legs. Her legs are wrapped around his back. This can be used for intercourse or close, sensual cuddling. If the goddess needs more yang stimulation of the clitoris, find a way to arrange for this. (A favorite position for many women is to lie facedown while he enters from behind— then the lingam comes into direct contact with the sacred spot, and she can use a hand under herself to add clitoral stimulation.) If he needs more yin energy, he should find a way to communicate this so that she can help him spread his energy and relax. All previous comments about connectedness, breathing, and visualization apply once again—only now there is no "leader." Be sure to have fun. Laughing can be appropriate and liberating!

Climaxing: Climax may take place separately or together, but either way, see if you can approach it slowly and deliberately, remembering to stay relaxed and to stay in touch with your breath, your heart, and your radiance (and those of your lover). Some well-timed words of love, appreciation, or imagery as your lover approaches orgasm can have a profound effect on the depth and intensity of the experience. Sounding (i.e., intentionally "singing" a prolonged tone) together also produces interesting effects and is highly recommended.

Resting and finishing: After he ejaculates (also if he chooses not to), stay for a while with lingam in yoni as it softens, and remain consciously connected, continuing to circulate your energies with your breath. You might imagine reversing the flow, so that the lingam is visualized as absorbing energy from the yoni: her breath sends energy from her heart down to her yoni, he inhales it into his lingam and up to his heart, then exhales it back into her heart. When you separate, it is another special moment, and an opportunity to acknowledge one another with a "Namaste" (bowing to each other with palms together), which signifies that the spirit in you honors the spirit in the other.

CLAIMING THE SACRED

I experienced Tantra as a reconnection with my female essence. I found that my Shakti was a treasure, something I had been vaguely aware of missing, but that I had had no map to lead me to until this system provided guidance. I love the goddess part of me. She gets to exert her power in the most loving way, she gets to be pampered on occasion, she can dance, laugh, tease, dress up, let go, and light up. She infuses my every day with warmth and generosity, and I still practice medicine and think cogently and clearly. She is part of my soul, rediscovered.

After David experienced Tantra for the first time, I overheard him talking to one of his close friends about the experience. He said, "I thought I went to learn about sex; instead, what I learned about was love." We continue to explore the limits, the rooms of this new house of connection, and we now feel that the reason there is continued fascination and growth in this sexual, transpersonal realm is because we are exploring the universe, the Divine in each other, which is endless.

10

A Final Note

MAGNIFICENT SEX FOR YOU

Multidimensional living is wonderful and energizing. It blossoms as you combine your strengths with your lover's. As you have gone through this book and evaluated your strong and weak dimensions, the areas where you are solid and the ones that need work, hopefully you have kept in mind that it is the relationship that we want to be multidimensional.

You do not have to be perfect in all the aspects of loving. You may be wonderful, a real natural, in the heart and intimacy dimensions, not afraid of abandonment or betrayal, ready to speak the truth and to commit to your mate. Or you may have the lust/desire dimension down pat, with a strong connection to your sexual power and to the sensual aspects of making love. Great!

The trick is to create a relationship that has all of the dimensions. Therefore, each of you has to value what the other brings to the sexual experience. Rather than criticizing or blaming your lover for not being like you, or responding as you would in a particular situation, you should thank your lover for his or her contribution whether it be lust or heart or soul, and then you contribute your strengths.

Women and men are held back from discovering the sacred in sex because of the habits, attitudes, and beliefs that hold them back in the seven dimensions. For example, a woman who has not accepted and embraced herself for who she is (who has blocks in the intimacy and aesthetic dimensions) will continue to feel unworthy to claim her goddess and will think it is impossible for someone like her even to strive for such a high goal. Now is the time to throw out those constrictive, restrictive attitudes. Promise yourself not to let false or outdated beliefs keep you from magnificient sex!

Now is a good time to review the seven dimensions:

1. During sex, does your body function physically the way you think it should?
2. Have you consciously pleasured your partner's body outside of sex in the last ten days?
3. Are you technically a better lover now than you were last year? Have you initiated sex in the past ten days?
4. Does your physical connection express the depth of your emotional commitment to your partner?
5. Have you revealed an internal "conversation" to your partner recently?
6. Have you made love unself-consciously in the last ten days?
7. Are you consciously striving for ecstatic lovemaking?

These questions correspond to each of the seven dimensions of sexual connection. And if you answered no to any of these questions, then that area or dimension of your sexual relationship probably needs work and attention. To realign the seven dimensions of your sexual relationship and achieve a blissful connection, you need to energize and sustain the positive aspect of all seven dimensions:

1. Become technically superior by understanding the biology and anatomy of your body.
2. Incorporate the play of the senses in your lovemaking and allow for more pleasure.
3. Celebrate the passionate, lustful connection and be willing to take the sexual self out of the closet.
4. Stay connected to each other's heart and exchange expressions of your love for one another.
5. Reveal the truth of who you are to your lover.
6. Risk showing your radiance and let go of your self-consciousness.
7. Expect the ecstatic and embrace the soulful when it occurs.

Magnificent sex requires a partnership. Here the whole is truly greater than the sum of the parts. This single step of appreciating your partner's strength can have a dramatic effect on the sexual battles that I often witness and am sometimes expected to referee.

Also, you can speak to your man or woman in their area of strength. Imagine this is like an overseas business. If you were going to develop a partnership in Japan, for example, you would probably go to the effort of learning some of the Japanese language and customs. You might learn about the custom of bowing: who bows first, how low do you bow, and who rises from the bow first. It is an important custom in that country. You wouldn't go there and say, "Bowing is stupid! I've never bowed to anybody in my entire life and I'm not about to start now," and expect to do much business in that country.

If your partner is a romantic and very connected to the heart dimension, someone who loves gifts and flowers, then you don't say, "Flowers, stupid flowers, they are expensive, they die in three days, I'm not going to buy any of those," and expect to do much business in that country! And if you have a lover who loves the desire dimension, who is connected to lusty, hot sex, then you might say "C'mon, big guy, I've got something in the bedroom to show you right now." That would certainly get his attention!

Of course, this is playing around with the dimensions, but it works better to speak to each other's strength rather than to berate your mate for a lack of skill or attachment to one of the seven areas.

Next, look at your sex life from the perspective of the entire seven dimensions. Are you missing something? Is one whole area gone, vanished, or never explored? Here is where you can have a joint project to bring this area into your connection. Sometimes, I see couples who are all about getting it on. They know how "to do" each other, they are technically good, but where is the awe, the radiance, the being-swept-away feeling? Then there are numerous partners who have deep affection and love for each other; they hold hands, they talk earnestly, they feel as if they are joined at the hip emotionally, but there is no sexual juice, lust, energy, or electricity. You may not be fighting about whose dimensional strengths are better because you share the same ones, but do you have all the aspects of loving represented? How could you possibly be satisfied with two-dimensional sex? It is not nearly as interesting as having the entire spectrum.

Remember, the vision of your good sex, GS, division can be whatever the two of you agree upon. So, when you cut your deal, include everything each of you wants. It is then a goal to work toward, to review, to mark your progress against. It is a cooperative venture instead of a blaming game. Admittedly, this new division is not something that you can directly will to your heirs or give to your friends, but all of those you love will be the beneficiaries of the rich, multidimensional fortune that you have created.

I believe that it is time we claimed all that we can be sexually. It's time that we not settle for less than what we deserve to have with our lover and soul mate. When we do this, we have an exceptional connection, magnificent sex, and the most exquisite gift we could ever present to our partner—

GIFT

What can I give you that you do not already possess?

What is mine that is not also yours?

What will have meaning to you that
matches your meaning to me?

Impoverished, I cast about for a tribute
to the man in my life for a quarter century.
A trip to a far, fragrant place?
An erotic automobile?
A sensual, sweeping piece of art?

Is there anything that will pierce
your heart to its core,
carrying my sweet poison
of love?

No, I decide,
this will have to be a far more
precious gift.

It will be my hand
when you are afraid.

It will be my smile
when you have lost touch
with your radiance.

It will be the blessing
of my sacred sexuality
bestowed upon your soul.

I have taken all the price tags off.

I hope you like it.

—To David from Lana

Resources: Medical Information and Sexuality References

MEDICAL INFORMATION

DRUGS THAT OFTEN CAUSE SEXUAL DYSFUNCTION

GENERIC NAME	BRAND NAME
ANTIARRHYTHMIA	
digoxin	*Lanoxin*
ANTIHYPERTENSIVE	
atenolol	*Tenormin*
chlorthalidone	*Hygroton, Thalitone*
clonidine	*Catapres*
hydrochlorothiazide	*Esidrix, HydroDiuril*
labetalol	*Normodyne, Trandate*
methyldopa	*Aldomet*
propranolol	*Inderal*
reserpine	*Serpalan*
spironolactone	*Aldactone*
ANTI-PARKINSON	
levodopa	*Dopar, Larodopa*
ANTISEIZURE	
carbamazepine	*Atretol, Tegretol*
phenytoin	*Dilantin*
primidone	*Myidone, Mysoline*
ANTIULCER	
cimetidine	*Tagamet, Tagamet HB*
CHOLESTEROL-LOWERING	
niacin	*Niacor, Nicolar*
statins	*Mevacor, Lipitor, Zocor*
ENDOMETRIOSIS	
danazol	*Danocrine*

GENERIC NAME	BRAND NAME

GLAUCOMA

dichlorphenamide	*Daranide*
methazolamide	*MZM, Neptazane*

PSYCHIATRIC PROBLEMS

Antianxiety

alprazolam	*Xanax*
diazepam	*Valium*

Antidepressant

clomipramine	*Anafranil*
fluoxetine	*Prozac*
imipramine	*Norfranil, Tofranil*
paroxetine	*Paxil*
phenelzine	*Nardil*
sertraline	*Zoloft*
trazodone	*Desyrel, Trazon*
venlafaxine	*Effexor*

Antipsychotic

chlorpromazine	*Thorazine, Thor-Prom*
fluphenazine	*Permitil, Prolixin*
lithium	*Eskalith, Lithonate*
thioridazine	*Mellaril*

SEXUALITY REFERENCES

BODY

Aldred, Caroline. *Divine Sex*. London: Carroll & Brown Limited, 1996. *A complete sexuality book on the Eastern approaches to loving.*

Barbach, Lonnie. *For Yourself*. New York: Doubleday/Signet, 1975. *Written fifteen years ago, but an excellent book on how to achieve orgasm.*

Heiman, Julia, Ph.D., and Joseph Lopiccolo, Ph.D. *Becoming Orgasmic*. New York: Prentice Hall Press, 1988. *Another detailed book on orgasmic response.*

Leiblum, Sandra R., and Raymond C. Rosen. *Sexual Desire Disorders*. New York: Guilford Press, 1988. *A comprehensive approach to theories regarding causes of decreased desire.*

Masters, William, Virginia Johnson, and Robert Kolodry. *Masters and Johnson on Sex & Human Loving*. Boston: Little Brown & Co., 1986. *From A to Z, human sexuality from the experts.*

Sevely, Josephine Lowndes. *Eve's Secrets*. New York: Random House, 1987. *New thoughts on female anatomy.*

Zilbergeld, B. *The New Male Sexuality*. New York: Bantam, 1992. *A great book on men's sexuality.*

MIND

Barbach, Lonnie. *For Each Other—Sharing Sexuality Intimacy*. New York: Doubleday/Signet, 1984. *Extensive information on sexuality and couples issues.*

Barbach, Lonnie. *Erotic Interludes, Pleasures: Women Write Erotica*. New York: Doubleday & Co., 1986. *Erotica written by women authors. Fun.*

Haffner, Debra. *From Diapers to Dating*. New York: Newmarket Press, 1999. *A great book on sexuality for parents.*

Neruda, Pablo. *100 Love Sonnets*. University of Texas Press, 1986. *A beautiful book of poetry in both English and sensual Spanish.*

Pearsall, Paul, Ph.D. *Sexual Healing*. New York: Crown, 1994. *Using the power of an intimate, loving relationship to heal your body and soul.*

Rako, Susan, M.D. *The Hormone of Desire: The Truth About Sexuality, Menopause, and Testosterone.* New York: Harmony Books, 1996. *The groundbreaking book that gives women and their doctors the opportunity to make informed decisions about testosterone deficiency and supplementation.*

Tiefer, Leonore. *Sex Is Not a Natural Act & Other Essays.* Westview Press, 1995.

Wolfe, Janet L., Ph.D. *What to Do When He Has a Headache.* New York: Penguin Books, 1992. *A common problem in midlife sexuality is when she wants it more than he does.*

SPIRIT

Anand, Margo. *The Art of Sexual Ecstasy.* Los Angeles: Jeremy P. Tarcher, Inc., 1989. *A beautiful, complete, and authoritative book about sexuality and spirituality.*

Mann, A. T., and Jane Lyle. *Sacred Sexuality.* Barnes & Noble, 1995. *A thorough discussion of the origins of sacred sex in a beautifully illustrated book.*

Moore, Rickie. *A Goddess in My Shoes.* Atlanta: Humanics New Age, 1988. *A straightforward, humorous account of the author's path toward self-knowledge, with exercises.*

Moore, Thomas. *The Soul of Sex.* HarperCollins Publishers, 1998. *Profound, thoughtful book on sexuality and soul.*

Muir, Charles, and Carolyn Muir. *Tantra, the Art of Conscious Loving.* San Francisco: Mercury House, 1989. *A good presentation of Tantra and its application to western love relationships.*

VIDEOS

Anand, Margo, et al. *Tantra: Ancient Secrets of Sexual Ecstasy for Modern Lovers.* Also *Multi Orgasmic Response Ecstasy Training for Women and Their Lovers,* and *Multi Orgasmic Response Ecstasy Training for Men and Their Lovers.* 1-800-9 TANTRA. *A comprehensive guide to the erotic arts of the East, and two wonderful instructional videos.*

Connop, Cynthia, and Christine Carter. *The Secrets of Sacred Sex.*
Healing Arts. 1-800-2 LIVING. *A guide to intimacy and loving.*

Holstein, Lana, M.D. *Sexuality and Vitality.* Canyon Ranch
Bookstore. 520-749-9000 x 380 *A video of my lecture on anatomy,
physiology, emotions, and spirituality.*

Muir, Charles, and Carolyn Muir. *Secrets of Female Sexual Fantasy.*
808-572-8364. *Now you can create Heaven on Earth in your love
life. Emphasizes the Sacred Spot massage.*

Muir, Charles, and Carolyn Muir. *Tantra: The Art of Conscious Loving.*
Hawaiian Goddess Video. 808-572-8364. *A modern approach to the
sacred Indian art of love.*

Scantling, Sandra. *Discovering Extraordinary Sex.* Sinclair Institute,
P.O. Box 8865, Chapel Hill, NC 27514. *Bring your relationship to a
new realm of excitement.*

Stubbs, Kenneth Ray. *Tantric Massage Video.* 1-800-9 TANTRA.
A comprehensive guide to the erotic arts of the East.

FUN SEX

Corn, Laura. *101 Nights of Grrreat Sex.* Park Avenue Publishing, 1995.
Great scenarios in a clever format—a bestseller.

Paget, Lou. *How to Be a Great Lover: Girlfriend-to-Girlfriend Totally
Explicit Techniques That Will Blow His Mind.* Broadway Books,
1999. *Just what it says. She also has a book for men.*

Scantling, Sandra. *Getting Creative with Sex.* Sinclair Institute, P.O.
Box 8865, Chapel Hill, NC 27514. *Explore new ways to add
excitement to your lovemaking.*

Shelburne, Walter A., Ph.D. *For Play: 150 Sex Games for Couples.*
Waterfall Press, 1993. *Self-explanatory; great ideas.*

Stubbs, Kenneth Ray, Ph.D. *Secret Sexual Positions: Ancient
Techniques for Modern Lovers.* Secret Garden, 1998. *Interesting,
with male and female comments.*

RESOURCES

The Kinsey Institute
Indiana University, Morrison Hall 313
Bloomfield, IN 47401-3700
Phone: (812) 855-7686
Fax: (812) 855-8277

SIECUS
130 W. 42nd St., Suite 350
New York, NY 10036
Phone: (212) 819-9770
Fax: (212) 819-9776

WWW.TANTRA.COM
Good Web site for sexuality and spirituality books/tapes/music.

About the Author

Dr. LANA L. HOLSTEIN is a nationally known expert in the field of sexuality and women's health. She did her undergraduate work at Stanford University and completed her medical training at Yale Medical School. In 1993, after fifteen years of a shared family practice with her husband in Flagstaff, Arizona, they moved to Tucson, where Dr. Holstein took the position of Director of Women's Health at Canyon Ranch, the renowned health resort in Arizona. For the past four years she has traveled widely in this country, giving keynote speaking presentations and workshops on women's health, hormone health and therapy, and sexuality to audiences of up to nine hundred women at a time, reaching thousands of women annually. Many of these guest appearances are part of the PBS-affiliated program *Speaking of Women's Health*. In addition, Dr. Holstein also regularly appears as a guest presenter at both scholarly and public forums.

Dr. Holstein's work with sexuality and women in midlife has been extensively quoted and referred to in many magazines, including *Prevention, Marie Claire, Ladies' Home Journal, Bride, American Health,* and *New Woman,* as well as in syndicated columns in newspapers and scholarly publications.

Dr. Holstein has informed *How to Have Magnificent Sex* with a scientific thoroughness and blended it with a personable, genuine voice that combines her knowledge as a physician, her wisdom as a counselor, and her passion as a sexual woman. Dr. Holstein opens the doors to ectstatic, spiritually based sexuality that bridges the gap for Western readers.